English
Liberalism
and the State

PROBLEMS IN EUROPEAN CIVILIZATION

Under the editorial direction of
John Ratte

English
Liberalism
and the State

Individualism or
Collectivism?

Edited and with an Introduction by

Harold J. Schultz
Bethel College, Kansas

D. C. HEATH AND COMPANY
Lexington, Massachusetts Toronto London

PREFACE

The collision of men and ideas creates much of the drama of history since ideas serve both as the vehicle for change and as an argument for continuity. In nineteenth-century England the interplay of ideas and men was particularly keen and the issues of consequence, not only to the Victorians, but to all succeeding generations.

Harold T. Parker of Duke University first spurred my interest in the problem this volume examines. Many colleagues and students offered their suggestions and assistance at various stages of the work. I am particularly indebted to Dwight E. Lee, former editor of the Problems in European Civilization series, and Maurice Shock of University College, Oxford University, for their reading of the manuscript and their careful criticisms. The need for such a volume—and the shape it actually took—grew out of the Social Science Honors Seminar at Stetson University, a course on Ideas and Men in Conflict in which students keep asking the questions that are raised by the contributors in the following selections.

H. J. S.

CONTENTS

III THE NEW LIBERALISM

IV THE VICTORIAN ADMINISTRATIVE STATE: A REAPPRAISAL

INTRODUCTION

There is no more fascinating theme in contemporary history than to follow the stages through which the laissez-faire *"night-watchman state" of the nineteenth century has been transformed into the "welfare state" of today —at one and the same time its logical opposite and its logical corollary.*

—*E. H. Carr*

The quotation above captures the peculiar paradox of nineteenth-century English liberalism. No philosophy of government was invoked more frequently by the Victorians or meant more different things to them. If liberalism meant laissez-faire individualism, how could it also spur state intervention? If it was equated with liberty, as it was, how could it endorse laws limiting freedom of action? No wonder the term almost defies definition and seems to suffer from such a serious case of intellectual incoherence. In 1848 the *Edinburgh Review* tried to define "a liberal system of government," only to find it quite impossible to characterize, let alone define, and finally admitted that "the phrase, we confess, is not very precise."

Its very imprecision is owing, in part, to the multiple origins and the lack of doctrinaire ideology that characterize English liberalism. One stream of political liberalism was introduced by Lilburne, Milton, and Locke in their seventeenth-century resistance to royal authority and their advocacy of freedom of conscience and of the press. The Whigs asserted their proprietary claim to this tradition after 1688, but their guardianship was largely an aristocratic and conserving one. This became conspicuous when the French Revolution made them suspicious of reform and frightened them into joining Pitt and the Tories. Only Charles James Fox and a few faithful followers upheld the liberties of the individual for the duration of the war with France.

The second—and greatest—chapter in English liberalism spans the century following the Congress of Vienna (1815–1914). The term "Liberal" became, in Spanish political circles, a nickname for the opponents of the reactionary Bourbon monarchy, and Elie Halévy, the noted French historian, claims that its currency was restored in England as an import from Spain. Such an import, if indeed it was, would have been merely an exotic term if it had not had the good fortune of providing an appealing formula for dealing with a new set of conditions which then prevailed. The industrial changes that were transforming the English economy were creating problems of an unprecedented nature. The prevailing ideologies and practices of a slow-changing agricultural and handicraft society could not cope with the new demands of industrialism, urbanization, and population growth. Nor were the new rich—the middle class—content with the inadequacies of the old order, whose mercantilist laws limited their profits and growth, and whose unreformed parliament prevented their political participation.

What was extraordinary was the manner in which the liberal solutions of the political economists and philosophical radicals (Benthamites) seemed to fit so perfectly both the self-interest and the moral principles of this new industrial class. A century ago Victor Hugo noted that "there is nothing more powerful than an idea whose time has come." If there was an opportune time and place for liberalism, it was nineteenth-century England. To give undue recognition to the force of ideas is, of course, to discount the equally important historical context within which the collision of men, ideas, and circumstances occurred and without which the ideas would have been both lonely and historically meaningless. But to minimize the remarkable influence that liberalism had on Victorian England would be equally unhistorical.

What was the appeal of this liberalism? What problems did it solve? What new problems did it create? In an age profoundly committed to reform rather than revolution, Victorians debated the relationship of the individual to the state and the role of the state in society. The problem of reconciling individualism and collectivism in a free society divided Victorians as it does us today.

Central to liberalism was the idea of freedom. The laissez-faire liberalism of Ricardo and the collectivist liberalism of Lloyd George differ radically in means, but the advocates of each position believed they were setting the individual free. Can freedom be provided by a variety of means, or do means determine ends? Such a problem is best examined, not by treating it abstractly or in a historical vacuum, but by catching the clash of political opinion that actually took place among English political theorists and politicians as they sought answers to what Burke rightly considered "one of the finest problems in legislation, namely, to determine what the State ought to take upon itself to direct by the public wisdom, and what it ought to leave, with as little interference as possible, to individual action."

Other problems we encounter today also have their counterpart in nineteenth-century England. What is the relationship of liberty and justice (two commonly held liberal values) to equality? Gladstone believed profoundly in the first two but noted that, unlike France, "of equality she [England] has never been much enamoured." But is a liberty which fails to provide equal opportunity really a human liberty? Or take the question of power. To take wealth away from the rich and concentrate it in the hands of the state means inevitably a concentration of power in the state. By removing the power of the factory owner to exploit the worker has society only replaced the tyranny of the industrial capitalist with the tyranny of the state or the tyranny of the majority? The essays in this volume cluster around these questions.

In answering them, differences in principle and practice stand out and dramatically reveal what the nineteenth century was the first to believe: that history is the story of change. Unlike the men of the eighteenth century, who could only speculate about the possibility of change, the Victorians not only knew that change was possible, but were exuberant about its possibilities. In their minds it was identified with that almost sacred word "progress." Queen Victoria's long reign, however, puts an illusory uniformity on this period of time in which ideas, values, and political practices changed profoundly. No ideology, in all its political economic, and social dimensions, changed more profoundly than did Victorian liberalism.

The metamorphosis of these nineteenth-century views on liberalism also illuminates one of the fundamental features of the historical process—the unpredictability of the ultimate consequence of an idea or course of action. As proposals for reform slip into the institutional life of Britain, they often do so in a final form quite different from the original proposal, or—to put it another way—political theorists plan, their plans make a difference in society, but not necessarily the difference planned. Bentham's theory of utility, for example, expounded in the support of individualism and freedom from governmental restrictions, is also invoked as the justification for an omnicompetent administrative state with virtually unlimited powers. Such shifts make the problem of comprehending the evolution of nineteenth-century thought one of the most troublesome encountered by students of history and the social sciences. Is not the "night-watchman state" the logical opposite of the "welfare state"? How then can the welfare state also be the "logical corollary" of the night-watchman state? Illuminating and unraveling this paradox is the primary function—and fascination—of the following readings.

Section I introduces the reader to the liberal assumptions held by the mid-Victorians. Underlying these assumptions was an intense belief in freedom, reason, individualism, and the inevitability of progress. This accent on individualism and freedom assumed that less law would provide more liberty; therefore a deep distrust of the power of the state was its natural corollary. Reform, in these terms, required no blueprint for a new society or more governmental services, but rather the freeing of the individual from restrictions, the manufacturer from artificial restraints on trade, and local government from centralization. At the international level freedom was equated with free trade, which, in turn, would free nations from empires, exploitation, and wars.

The industrial middle class, in an uneasy alliance with the Whigs, provided the chief source of support for English liberalism. By 1832 sufficient members of the landed aristocracy sensed the need of aligning the new wealthy class with them, rather than against them. The Whig leadership invoked the "principles of 1688" and introduced the Great Reform Bill as a rational measure, rather than a democratic one, preferring reform from above to revolution from below.[1] It was Gladstone who finally fused the old Whigs, the new middle class, and moral liberalism into a powerful combination before fragmenting it over the issue of Irish Home Rule.

Liberalism acquired its views on the state and society largely from two schools: the classical economists and the philosophical radicals. David Ricardo's "natural laws," along with the corollary theses of Adam Smith and Thomas Malthus, justified and sanctified the practices of the new factory capitalists who saw in the iron law of wages an escape from the encumbering and obsolete laws of a preindustrial society and a justification for subsistence wages. Neither laborer nor government should tamper with these immutable economic laws, not even to relieve miseries, declared Ricardo.

Complementing Ricardo's laissez-faire views on economics and the role of government was Jeremy Bentham's rational principle of utility. Like the classical economists, Bentham saw no conflict between an individual's self-interested pursuit of his own ends and the interests of the community. Why? Because the interest of the community was merely "the sum of the interests of the several members who compose it," and therefore the best service that the government could render to agriculture, commerce, and manufacturing was to stand out of the way.

Bentham's principles provided liberalism with a working intellectual structure that it previously had lacked, and his ideas became one of the drive shafts for renovating, rather than repudiating, existing institutions. But can one measure happiness in Bentham's quantitative fashion? Is it true that self-interest is generally as enlightened as Ricardo and Bentham argue, and that such enlightened self-interest always operates in the public interest? If it is in the self-interest of the factory owner to exploit his workers, is this also in the public interest?

Self-help is the answer offered by Samuel Smiles since even "the best institutions can give a man no active help." His accent on individualism and his confidence in "the virtues of industry, frugality, temperance and honesty" gave English liberalism its buoyant and optimistic thrust and attracted Englishmen who were suspicious of

[1] See Gilbert A. Cahill, *The Great Reform Bill of 1832, Problems in European Civilization* (Lexington, Mass.: D. C. Heath and Co., 1969).

"French" abstractions and first principles. For Smiles the state was little more than a god of the gaps whose function it was to fill in areas not manned by individual effort. Was not such liberal ideology merely an escape from responsibility for poverty and squalor on the grounds that intervention would tamper with natural laws of individual initiative?

Such a charge might hold if liberalism were shorn of its moral dimension. No one in Victorian England embodied this dimension of liberalism more eloquently or effectively than W. E. Gladstone, four times Liberal prime minister of England. With Gladstone the facile optimism of early liberalism is gone. Even though he professed and practiced the liberal creed of peace, economy, and reform, in the final analysis, his policies were based on the moral imperatives of justice and liberty, even when such policies were politically disastrous, as they were in the case of Irish Home Rule. Unlike Ricardo, Gladstone did not hesitate to use the state to extend political freedom, and reluctantly he accepted the inevitability of democracy. "Decision by majorities," he observed, "is as much an expedient as lighting by gas. In adopting it as a rule we are not realizing perfection but bowing to an imperfection."[2]

What had been achieved under such men and policies was impressive. The catalogue of benefits was long, and credit for them belongs to a large degree to individuals following their own conscience and interests. But did the new freedom for some individuals and sectors of society mean freedom for all, and was the competition truly fair and free, as Ricardo claimed? The first principle of laissez-faire liberalism, and the moral convictions that motivated it, rested upon an affirmative answer.

The essentially negative reforms of laissez-faire and utilitarian liberalism helped to abolish the corn laws and political and religious disabilities; at the same time their efforts prompted increased governmental efficiency and centralization. Thereafter liberal reformers could not agree on their future course of action. How should they approach the glaring economic and social evils that remained? A new factor complicated the picture—the extension of the franchise

[2] John Morley, *The Life of W. E. Gladstone,* 3 volumes (London: Macmillan and Comp., Ltd., 1903), Vol. III, p. 123.

to the masses. Liberalism, with its middle-class virtues and sensitivities to the inviolability of property and contract, was not as appealing to the working classes, for whom the liberal doctrine meant,
too often, the freedom to work long hours at low pay.

Changing conditions were also recasting the economic and political realities of England. By 1870 free trade had sacrificed British
agricultural interests to the expansion of industrialism. The country
squires, for economic reasons and by social conviction, were natural
critics of the industrial capitalists. The depressions of the 1870's and
1880's also ended the golden years of Victorian capitalism. The results of investigations showed that the squalor and other social consequences of unregulated industrialism threatened not only the poor,
but also the very industrialization that had spawned these conditions.
At the same time the Second Reform Act (1867) enfranchised a considerable portion of the urban working classes, whose interests were
not the same as those of their employers. Better wages and conditions of employment would come for them through collective
bargaining, not through freedom of contract. The identification of
liberalism with a single economic and social interest was no longer
adequate. Could middle-class liberalism broaden its base in time to
encompass the newly enfranchised workers and become the creed
of the masses? What reformulations would be necessary? The selections in Section II focus on the problems and political theories of
liberalism in flux.

In the first reading, E. H. Carr proceeds to undermine the moral
foundations of laissez-faire liberalism, which assumed that "natural"
rewards and punishments would follow from the free and fair competition of individuals in the market place. Carr claims that once the
myth of equal opportunity is exploded, it erodes Smiles's or Gladstone's moral argument for the nonintervention of state in society.

Must the natural order of economic society be devoid of justice
and ethics? Are there no philosophical or political defenses against
the social destructiveness that accompanies unregulated industrialism? The transitional figure whose finely tuned moral sensitivities
rescued utilitarianism from its rigid and amoral calculation of pleasure and pain was John Stuart Mill. His redefinition of liberalism
focused on intellectual and moral freedom, but moved to the external
threats to freedom. The greatest of these threats was not govern-

ment, but an intolerant society that would crush all nonconformity and diversity. Nevertheless, Mill never could resolve the liberal antithesis between the individual and the state so that he could enlarge upon the relationship between freedom and social responsibility. The reader is led to the threshold, but not over.

If Mill moved cautiously and pessimistically into the future, it was, in part, because he saw that the ever-increasing problems of urbanization and industrialization could not be resolved merely by economic growth or through political mechanisms. A mood of doubt and introspection replaced the earlier liberal certainties. Significantly, it was men of ideas and property, whose consciences had been pricked by social ills, who were challenging from within the established orthodoxies. Some liberals, like Mill, attempted to come to terms with the new egalitarian forces that were pressing for their due; others, like Robert Lowe, fought the trend. Lowe was no defender of a static constitution, but progress, he argued, was related to the quality of the voter. One man should not mean, *ipso facto,* one vote.

Lowe, with his "inexpressible admiration" for middle-class liberalism, based on a limited and intelligent electorate, is mocked for his philistine values in the essay by Matthew Arnold. Along with his fellow critics, Carlyle and Ruskin, Arnold indicted the "anarchy" of laissez-faire liberalism, not on economic or rational grounds, but for moral and artistic reasons. The whole liberal doctrine seemed unjust, unlovely, and culturally tasteless. To Arnold, the Nonconformists[3] were the uncultured who turned liberalism into a Protestant philistinism. To Gladstone they were "the backbone of British Liberalism." For John F. Glaser, nineteenth-century liberalism and Nonconformity were so inseparable that "when the iron went out of the soul of Nonconformity," not only was the dynamism of liberalism lost, but "the decline of Nonconformity had as an inevitable consequence the decline of Liberalism."

By the 1870's most of the religious and political disabilities imposed in the seventeeth century on the Protestant groups outside the Church of England had been removed. Flourishing among the middle class that was rising to industrial and political power, Non-

[3] See the footnote on page 43 for the theological spectrum embraced by Nonconformity and the various terms used to identify it.

conformity easily identified itself with liberal ideology and Gladstone's Liberal party. Were these Dissenters already too obviously identified with the middle class to influence the working classes who were awakening to political consciousness? Does the decline of Dissent signal the decline of liberalism, as Glaser argues, or was political liberalism already in trouble before the decline of Dissent at the beginning of the twentieth century?

One Dissenter who did capture Nonconformist and working-class support was Joseph Chamberlain. While Mill professed the need for redistributing the wealth and proffered a tentative program for bridging the gap between the "haves" and the "have nots," Chamberlain practiced in Birmingham what Mill preached. "I believe," said Chamberlain, "that the great evil with which we have to deal is the excessive inequality in the distribution of riches." Assisted by leading Nonconformist ministers, Chamberlain transformed Birmingham by a program of public ownership and social welfare. His success on the municipal level paved the way for making positive social reform an essential part of a new national liberalism.

What made Chamberlain's brand of "socialism" increasingly palatable to English liberalism? Was it its lack of doctrinaire ideology or its accent on social justice that made it seem more humanitarian than collectivist? Or did the shift in political power from property owners to the nonpossessing class make Chamberlain's assault on property appear as political opportunism?

The last significant effort to stem the tide of "collectivism" and resuscitate laissez-faire individualism was made by Herbert Spencer. The selection by George Sabine dissects Spencer's conception of Social Darwinism, whose iron law of evolution had replaced Ricardo's iron law of wages. The reader may question Sabine's conclusion that the "philosophies of Mill and Spencer taken together left the theory of liberalism in a state of unintelligible confusion," but there is little question that this was indeed a period of flux and that liberalism was left divided and confused. What was evidently lacking was a fresh and positive view of freedom that could undergird the democratization of society and illuminate its function in government.

The seminal thinker who tilted the conventional liberal view of the state from one of suspicion to one of open acceptance of the state as an agent that would contribute to "positive freedom" was the Oxford don, Thomas Hill Green. His reformulation abolished the sharp line created by the classical economists between economics and politics, and inculcated a new moral idealism into liberalism. Starting with the centrality of society, in which the individual finds his fullest freedom—instead of with the individual, to whom government and society must adjust—Green offered a controversial reversal of priorities for liberals. Was it revolutionary in the modern sense or in the ancient sense—a full-circle return to the philosophy of the *polis*?

In the last reading of Section II Crane Brinton analyzes this interpretation of freedom and natural rights that challenged the premises of traditional English liberalism. Spencer saw in Green's vision of the state the death of liberalism. Brinton regards Green as "one of the saviours of Liberalism." The reader may have his own judgment to make after comparing their respective arguments.

If Mill provided the first significant reformulation of nineteenth-century liberalism, Green's restatement introduced the next phase in its metamorphosis. This transition was neither dramatic nor sudden. As Sabine reminds the student in his *History of Political Theory,* "The major purpose of his revision was to force the state into lines of legislation from which it had previously abstained on principles avowedly liberal."

Toward the end of the century it was becoming increasingly clear that neither the newly enfranchised workers nor public opinion would countenance a political philosophy that gave the government only a negative role in society. Nor would the new generation of liberals countenance such a doctrine. The change in the philosophical assumptions of liberalism were based, in part, on the political facts of life. The second and third reform acts ended the upper-middle-class electoral monopoly. Thereafter political success, indeed survival, seemed to depend upon the ability to appeal to the propertyless, working-class voter. Political democracy was leading, almost inevitably it seemed, to economic and social democracy. These facts, along with the new conditions of organized violence, congestion, and economic collectivism, demanded new forms of economic and social organization fundamentally different from the item-by-item reform measures of the earlier Victorians.

New administrative practices and legislative programs were in operation that corresponded to no particular philosophy of government. Perhaps this was because the trend to state intervention had been so gradual. As the *Economist* observed in 1895, "Little by little, year by year, the fabric of the State expenditure and State responsibility is built up like a coral island, cell on cell." Was this build-up, in fact, either inevitable or "year by year"?

The selections in Section III focus on the attempts to articulate new liberal formulas to correspond to the new practices and circumstances. One of the chief obstacles to acceptance of an expanding role for the state was the old liberal antithesis between the individual and the state. Its replacement by a broader concept of freedom was essential if liberalism was to continue as a working philosophy in British political life. In the last section, Green had pushed aside this stumbling block; in the first reading of Section III, D. G. Ritchie removed it altogether. The liberal habit of looking at the state as an element opposed to the individual is most inadequate for understanding the duties of government, Ritchie contended, since "the State and the individual are not sides of an antithesis between which we must choose. . . ." The two can grow greater—or diminish—together.

Within the Liberal party Herbert Samuel provided the definitive statement of the new liberalism, which the Liberal party attempted to implement in office after 1905. Like Green, Samuel insisted on an ethical dimension in liberalism. The moral duty of man and the state was to help all individuals achieve a good life. Using this prescription, Samuel and his party colleagues wrote a legislative program of social reform based on the rational, reformist inclinations of the nineteenth century.

With the benefit of hindsight the reader may ask if the Liberal party took the right model for interpreting twentieth-century society. Could a rational and ameliorative policy of social reform cope with the violence and social tensions of urban industrialism? At stake were the fundamental assertions of Lockian liberalism, with its accent on the individual, reason, and property—assertions which were products of a preindustrial and predemocratic society. How meaningful were these values in an industrial, propertyless, mass society that was increasingly motivated by the irrational?

One of the most dynamic and ambitious political practitioners of Samuel's new liberalism was David Lloyd George, who saw in the popular appeal of social reform an opportunity for himself and the Liberal party. Carrying on the radical tradition of Chamberlain, Lloyd George displays in the third reading why he was known as the "man of the people." By playing on their emotions and endorsing the new egalitarian emphasis in liberalism at the expense of traditional rights, Lloyd George grasped the political, if not the philosophical, implications of man's irrational needs.

"Equality of opportunity" became the platform of Lloyd George, and this demanded state intervention to make such social freedom possible. Freedom from destitution and freedom from unemployment required new programs, which could only be realized by legislating for social security. The Old Age Pensions Act (1908) and the National Insurance Act (1911) were legislative landmarks of this new emphasis on economic and social democracy. By asserting that state aid was a "right" rather than a "charity," these acts marked a historic break with the principle underlying the Poor Law of 1834. To the traditionalists they sounded the death knell of self-reliance.

The fourth and fifth selections expand the new accent on collectivism. Society was seen less as a mechanism and more as an organism. This change was due both to the reappraisal of the relation of the individual to his community in a mass democracy and to the increased prestige of biology in political thought. Spencer had introduced this alliance between biology and politics, seeing in it an argument for individualism. Hobson and Hobhouse used the same analogy to develop a collectivist philosophy of society. If the analogy of the living organism to society has any value, is it in reinforcing individualism or collectivism?

Were the old models and tools of the classical economists now obsolete in a world of Big Business, Big Finance, and Big Labor, as Hobson argued? If so, did it necessarily follow that liberals must substitute an organic policy of social reconstruction? As Hobson's reformulation moves liberalism toward a socialist ideology, the reader will need to assess the legitimacy of the distinctions Hobson has made between liberalism and socialism.

L. T. Hobhouse based his highly acclaimed formulation of liberalism on the social individual who constantly expands his freedom by growth. Such growth demanded state intervention, since freedom for one individual or group rests upon a corresponding restraint upon other individuals or groups. This position broke sharply with older liberalism, which assumed that freedom grew as restraints were lifted. The basic assumption of the philosophical radicals was that there was a natural harmony of interests between the self and the community. But Hobhouse asserted that, as experience had shown, what was good for the individual was not necessarily in the best interests of all. Therefore the social (or state) employment of proper restraints on freedom was in order.

The reader must determine whether Hobhouse characterizes a uniquely liberal welfare state, lying between laissez-faire liberalism on the one hand and doctrinaire socialism on the other hand, that achieves the advantages of each without their respective weaknesses. Or is Hobhouse's version of liberalism only a halfway house to socialism?

The next to the last selection, by Graham Wallas, reflects the influence of liberalism far beyond the confines of the Liberal party. The importance of his reconstruction of liberalism rests on the attempt to comprehend the reality of the irrational in human behavior. What Wallas feared was the despair that seemed to be engulfing liberals as they found their rational and optimistic assumptions unable to comprehend or to cope with irrational forces or fears. If democratic government rested upon government by reason, was not the validity of democracy at stake? Wallas countered by making his central point: to make democracy function in such a world, liberals must recognize and identify irrational factors so that rational and humane individuals can give leadership to the irrational forces in society.

Was Wallas one of the few liberals of his time to grasp the phenomenon of a mass urban democracy? Like other liberals, Wallas valued liberty more highly than democracy. Only those elements in democracy that enhanced individuality were to be defended. He was always aware of the "difficult task of adjusting the vastness of the Great Society to the smallness of individual men"—a task by no means resolved in the "Great Society" of contemporary America— but he was equally aware that no other political model offered as liberal a social organization as did democracy.

The final selection in Section III disputes the influence of Green and "Liberal-Hegelian" thought on early Fabian political ideology. The dispute between liberals and socialists, says A. M. McBriar, "is really a dispute about means rather than ends. . . ." As the reader examines this essay, he should be looking for the interaction of liberalism and Fabianism and the influence of one on the other. What were their essential differences, if any? If social reform made the new liberalism palatable to millions of Englishmen, did Fabianism make socialism sufficiently "English," as McBriar claims, to "enable a churchwarden, or an English trade unionist, to call himself a Socialist"?

While arguments for and against state intervention waxed and waned, the Victorian administrative state simply kept growing. This growth in power and complexity created, in turn, a growing army of administrators and experts. How did this Victorian administrative revolution take place? In what ways did Bentham shape its development? How compatible is the bureaucratic state with professed liberal principles? The two selections in Section IV are representative of the lively contemporary interest in this controversy, an interest especially keen since so many of the problems we face now, such as the wide discretionary powers granted to administrators and technicians, had their origins in nineteenth-century England.

The first selection is a debate between Oliver MacDonagh and Henry Parris on Bentham's influence as an architect of the Victorian state. Complicating the controversy over Bentham is the fact that he is invoked as the archetype of both laissez-faire individualism and the interventionist state. Does Parris provide an answer to the seeming paradox of the laissez-faire–state intervention controversy when he contends that the "question was then, as indeed it is today, not *laissez-faire* or State intervention, but where, in the light of constantly changing circumstances, the line between them should be drawn"?

The final selection focuses on the importance of the pioneer administrator or expert, such as Edwin Chadwick, in building the "social policy that led to the creation of the State as we know it nowadays in Britain." To what extent was the metamorphosis of the Victorian state due to the specific efforts of individuals responding to "the pressure of circumstances" rather than to the coherent policy of any party or to the ideas of liberalism or any other philosophy? Was the new shape of the state more or less inevitable, regardless of men or ideas? Without a Bentham or his determined disciple, Chadwick, would the story have been largely the same? For G. Kitson Clark, "something resembling what did happen would have happened, whoever the agents . . . might have been."

The advent of World War I unleashed such passions and violence that liberalism and the questions it spoke to seemed either obsolete or irrelevant. But the lamps of liberalism were not extinguished. Its principles were too basic to the human spirit to be permanently dimmed. The diverse interpretations of these principles offered in this book only underline the fact that liberalism was, and is, much more than a problem in the mechanics of political organization. It is a recognition of the uniqueness of the individual and of the necessity of social, economic, and political freedom for human fulfillment. Since liberalism is not a self-contained and static creed, but a value system based on freedom, its capacity to adjust to changing conditions is a sign of vitality that permits the expansion of freedom. Therefore the continual reworking or reformulation of liberalism is as essential to the future of freedom as is the belief in the worth of freedom.

The readings keep raising the questions that are critical to the survival of a free society. The reader will find far less agreement in the answers of the contributors than on the questions they raise. That is why it is important to keep raising these questions, Kitson Clark warns; for if we do not, the liberal states will succumb to totalitarianism:

There is, however, I believe, one condition for their survival. Something of the nature and history of these values and of the principles upon which they have been based must continue to be understood by the ordinary educated man. If that is crowded out of his education and consciousness then those values will be crowded out of a world, which will very speedily forget them as if they had never been.[4]

This volume is an attempt to identify and interpret the values and principles of liberalism so that they are not crowded out of our education and our world. How well these ideas and principles still speak to our kind of world is for the reader to determine.

[4] G. Kitson Clark, "The Modern State and Modern Society: Historic Tendencies and Future Probabilities," *Proceedings of the Royal Institute of Great Britain*, Vol. XXXVII (1959), p. 565. Cited by permission of the author.

Conflict of Opinion

Like all other contracts, wages should be left to the fair and free competition of the market, and should never be controlled by the interference of the legislature.

DAVID RICARDO

What ultimately discredited the philosophy . . . was the realization that the competitors did not start free and equal and that, the longer the competition continued, the less scope was left for freedom and equality, so that the moral foundation on which *laissez-faire* rested was more and more hopelessly undermined.

EDWARD H. CARR

Moreover, it is every day becoming more clearly understood, that the function of Government is negative and restrictive, rather than positive and active; being resolvable principally into protection—protection of life, liberty, and property.

SAMUEL SMILES

. . . freedom is only one side of social life. Mutual aid is not less important than mutual forbearance, the theory of collective action no less fundamental than the theory of personal freedom.

LEONARD T. HOBHOUSE

The community is a fictitious *body*, composed of the individual persons who are considered as constituting as it were its *members*. The interest of the community then is, what?—the sum of the interests of the several members who compose it.

JEREMY BENTHAM

. . . it is only the community acting as a whole that can possibly deal with evils so deep-seated as those to which I have referred.

JOSEPH CHAMBERLAIN

He [Mill] urged the primary value of spontaneity in the development of the individual, but he was content to see the state and society as enemies, rather than the agents, of free choice.

JOHN WESLEY DERRY

The State and the individual are not sides of an antithesis between which we must choose. . . .

DAVID G. RITCHIE

Liberalism, indeed, is no stereotyped collection of fixed proposals. It is a living force that applies itself in turn to all the changing phases of national life. . . .

HERBERT L. SAMUEL

I THE LIBERAL ASSUMPTIONS

David Ricardo
LAISSEZ-FAIRE IS A NATURAL LAW

David Ricardo (1772–1823), the son of a Dutch-Jewish banker, retired at the age of forty-two after making his fortune on the London Stock Exchange. Three years later (1817) his difficult study in theoretical economics was published. Its laissez-faire doctrine became immediately popular among the middle-class manufacturers who wished to escape from laws oriented to a preindustrial society. The "scientific" inevitability of his gloomy formulations dominated economic thought for the next forty years and made Ricardo the most influential of the classical economists. His deductions divorced economics from government and caused political economy to be known as the dismal science. In the following selection Ricardo deals with the "natural laws" by which wages are determined.

On Wages

Labour, like all other things which are purchased and sold, and which may be increased or diminished in quantity, has its natural and its market price. The natural price of labour is that price which is necessary to enable the labourers, one with another, to subsist and to perpetuate their race, without either increase or diminution.

The power of the labourer to support himself, and the family which may be necessary to keep up the number of labourers, does not depend on the quantity of money which he may receive for wages, but on the quantity of food, necessaries, and conveniences become essential to him from habit which that money will purchase. The natural price of labour, therefore, depends on the price of food, necessaries, and conveniences required for the support of the labourer and his family. With a rise in the price of food and necessaries, the natural price of labour will rise; with the fall in their price, the natural price of labour will fall.

* * *

The market price of labour is the price which is really paid for it, from the natural operation of the proportion of the supply to the demand; labour is dear when it is scarce and cheap when it is

From David Ricardo, *On the Principles of Political Economy and Taxation*, 3rd ed. (London: John Murray, 1821), pp. 86, 87–88, 94–95, 101–102. Reprinted by permission of John Murray, Publishers.

3

plentiful. However much the market price of labour may deviate from its natural price, it has, like commodities, a tendency to conform to it.

It is when the market price of labour exceeds its natural price that the condition of the labourer is flourishing and happy, that he has it in his power to command a greater proportion of the necessaries and enjoyments of life, and therefore to rear a healthy and numerous family. When, however, by the encouragement which high wages give to the increase of population, the number of labourers is increased, wages again fall to their natural price, and indeed from a reaction sometimes fall below it.

When the market price of labour is below its natural price, the condition of the labourers is most wretched: then poverty deprives them of those comforts which custom renders absolute necessaries. It is only after their privations have reduced their number, or the demand for labour has increased, that the market price of labour will rise to its natural price, and that the labourer will have the moderate comforts which the natural rate of wages will afford.

*   *   *

With a population pressing against the means of subsistence, the only remedies are either a reduction of people or a more rapid accumulation of capital. In rich countries, where all the fertile land is already cultivated, the latter remedy is neither very practicable nor very desirable, because its effect would be, if pushed very far, to render all classes equally poor. But in poor countries, where there are abundant means of production in store, from fertile land not yet brought into cultivation, it is the only safe and efficacious means of removing the evil, particularly as its effect would be to elevate all classes of the people.

*   *   *

These, then, are the laws by which wages are regulated, and by which the happiness of far the greatest part of every community is governed. Like all other contracts, wages should be left to the fair and free competition of the market, and should never be controlled by the interference of the legislature.

Jeremy Bentham
THE TEST OF UTILITY

Perhaps no other single theory was as influential as utilitarianism in bringing about item-by-item reform in nineteenth-century England. Its author, Jeremy Bentham (1748–1832), advocated the reform of virtually all the institutions of English life. To each institution he addressed two questions: Utility for what? Utility for whom? Each institution or custom should be continuously re-examined to see if it provided happiness—according to his quantitative measure of pleasures and pains—for the many or for the few. If Bentham's influence was important to English liberalism, was it as the advocate of laissez-faire individualism or as the architect of the interventionist state? His philosophy was later invoked to justify both individualism and collectivism. The following selections from A Fragment on Government (1776) and A Manual of Political Economy (1798) illustrate his utilitarian principles and their application to the government's function in the economy.

(I)

Of the Principle of Utility

1. Nature has placed mankind under the governance of two sovereign masters, *pain* and *pleasure*. It is for them alone to point out what we ought to do, as well as to determine what we shall do. On the one hand the standard of right and wrong, on the other the chain of causes and effects, are fastened to their throne. They govern us in all we do, in all we say, in all we think: every effort we can make to throw off our subjection, will serve but to demonstrate and confirm it. In words a man may pretend to abjure their empire: but in reality he will remain subject to it all the while. The *principle of utility* recognizes this subjection, and assumes it for the foundation of that system, the object of which is to rear the fabric of felicity by the hands of reason and of law. Systems which attempt to question it, deal in sounds instead of senses, in caprice instead of reason, in darkness instead of light.

But enough of metaphor and declamation: it is not by such means that moral science is to be improved.

(I) From Jeremy Bentham, *A Fragment on Government and An Introduction to the Principles of Morals and Legislation* (Oxford: Basil Blackwell, 1948), pp. 125–127. (II) From John Bowring (ed.), *Bentham's Works,* 11 volumes (Edinburgh: William Tait, 1843), Vol. III, pp. 33–35.

2. The principle of utility is the foundation of the present work: it will be proper therefore at the outset to give an explicit and determinate account of what is meant by it. By the principle of utility is meant that principle which approves or disapproves of every action whatsoever, according to the tendency which it appears to have to augment or diminish the happiness of the party whose interest is in question: or, what is the same thing in other words, to promote or to oppose that happiness. I say of every action whatsoever; and therefore not only of every action of a private individual, but of every measure of government.

3. By utility is meant that property in any object, whereby it tends to produce benefit, advantage, pleasure, good, or happiness, (all this in the present case comes to the same thing) or (what comes again to the same thing) to prevent the happening of mischief, pain, evil, or unhappiness to the party whose interest is considered: if that party be the community in general, then the happiness of the community: if a particular individual, then the happiness of that individual.

4. The interest of the community is one of the most general expressions that can occur in the phraseology of morals: no wonder that the meaning of it is often lost. When it has a meaning, it is this. The community is a fictitious *body,* composed of the individual persons who are considered as constituting as it were its *members.* The interest of the community then is, what?—the sum of the interests of the several members who compose it.

5. It is in vain to talk of the interest of the community, without understanding what is the interest of the individual. A thing is said to promote the interest, or to be *for* the interest, of an individual, when it tends to add to the sum total of his pleasures: or, what comes to the same thing, to diminish the sum total of his pains.

6. An action then may be said to be conformable to the principle of utility, or, for shortness sake, to utility, (meaning with respect to the community at large) when the tendency it has to augment the happiness of the community is greater than any it has to diminish it.

7. A measure of government (which is but a particular kind of action, performed by a particular person or persons) may be said to be conformable to or dictated by the principle of utility, when in

like manner the tendency which it has to augment the happiness of the community is greater than any which it has to diminish it.

8. When an action, or in particular a measure of government, is supposed by a man to be comformable to the principle of utility, it may be convenient, for the purposes of discourse, to imagine a kind of law or dictate, called a law or dictate of utility; and to speak of the action in question, as being conformable to such law or dictate.

9. A man may be said to be a partizan of the principle of utility, when the approbation or disapprobation he annexes to any action, or to any measure, is determined by and proportioned to the tendency which he conceives it to have to augment or to diminish the happiness of the community: or in other words, to its conformity or unconformity to the laws or dictates of utility.

10. Of an action that is conformable to the principle of utility one may always say either that it is one that ought to be done, or at least that it is not one that ought not to be done. One may say also, that it is right it should be done; at least that it is not wrong it should be done: that it is right action; at least that it is not a wrong action. When thus interpreted, the words *ought,* and *right* and *wrong,* and others of that stamp, have a meaning: when otherwise, they have none.

(II)

The practical questions, therefore, are how far the end in view is best promoted by individuals acting for themselves? and in what cases these ends may be promoted by the hands of government?

With the view of causing an increase to take place in the mass of national wealth, or with a view to increase of the means either of subsistence or enjoyment, without some special reason, the general rule is, that nothing ought to be done or attempted by government. The motto, or watchword of government, on these occasions, ought to be—*Be quiet.*

For this quietism there are two main reasons:

1. Generally speaking, any interference for this purpose on the part of government is needless. The wealth of the whole com-

munity is composed of the wealth of the several individuals belonging to it taken together. But to increase his particular portion is, generally speaking, among the constant objects of each individual's exertions and care. Generally speaking, there is no one who knows what is for your interest so well as yourself—no one who is disposed with so much ardour and constancy to pursue it.

2. Generally speaking, it is moreover likely to be pernicious, viz. by being unconducive, or even obstructive, with reference to the attainment of the end in view. Each individual bestowing more time and attention upon the means of preserving and increasing his portion of wealth, than is or can be bestowed by government, is likely to take a more effectual course than what, in his instance and on his behalf, would be taken by government.

It is, moreover, universally and constantly pernicious in another way, by the restraint or constraint imposed on the free agency of the individual. . . .

. . . With few exceptions, and those not very considerable ones, the attainment of the maximum of enjoyment will be most effectually secured by leaving each individual to pursue his own maximum of enjoyment, in proportion as he is in possession of the means. Inclination in this respect will not be wanting on the part of any one. Power, the species of power applicable to this case—viz. wealth, pecuniary power—could not be given by the hand of government to one, without being taken from another; so that by such interference there would not be any gain of power upon the whole.

The gain to be produced in this article by the interposition of government, respects principally the head of knowledge. There are cases in which, for the benefit of the public at large, it may be in the power of government to cause this or that portion of knowledge to be produced and diffused, which, without the demand for it produced by government, would either not have been produced, or would not have been diffused.

We have seen above the grounds on which the general rule in this behalf—*Be quiet*—rests. Whatever measures, therefore, cannot be justified as exceptions to that rule, may be considered as *non agenda* on the part of government. The art, therefore, is reduced within a small compass: *security* and *freedom* are all that industry requires. The request which agriculture, manufactures and commerce present to governments, is modest and reasonable as that which Diogenes made to Alexander: *"Stand out of my sunshine."* We have no need of favour—we require only a secure and open path.

Samuel Smiles
THE VIRTUE OF SELF-HELP

Dr. Samuel Smiles (1812–1904), a Leeds radical, popularized the prototype of mid-Victorian liberalism with his best-selling books, Self-Help *(1859) and* Thrift *(1875). Lessons in moral character and in the virtue of industry were drawn from his "Horatio Alger" stories of men who had risen from rags to riches by their own efforts. This gospel of self-help was the formula for working-class improvement. Smiles was probably the first writer to characterize the British tradition of freedom as "individualism." His injunctions endorsing self-help reinforced the liberal view of the state as simply "the reflex of the individuals composing it." The case for laissez-faire liberalism offered by Smiles should be compared with the counterarguments presented in Edward H. Carr's essay.*

"Heaven helps those who help themselves," is a well-tried maxim, embodying in a small compass the results of vast human experience. The spirit of self-help is the root of all genuine growth in the individual; and, exhibited in the lives of many, it constitutes the true source of national vigor and strength. Help from without is often enfeebling in its effect, but help from within invariably invigorates. Whatever is done *for* men or classes, to a certain extent takes away the stimulus and necessity of doing for themselves; and where men are subjected to over-guidance and over-government, the inevitable tendency is to render them comparatively helpless.

Even the best institutions can give a man no active help. Perhaps the most they can do is, to leave him free to develop himself and

From Samuel Smiles, *Self-Help* (New York: A. L. Burt, n.d.), pp. 1–3, 5–6, 277–278.

improve his individual condition. But in all times men have been prone to believe that their happiness and well-being were to be secured by means of institutions rather than by their own conduct. Hence the value of legislation as an agent in human advancement has usually been much over-estimated. To constitute the millionth part of a Legislature, by voting for one or two men once in three or five years, however conscientiously this duty may be performed, can exercise but little active influence upon any man's life and character. Moreover, it is every day becoming more clearly understood, that the function of Government is negative and restrictive, rather than positive and active; being resolvable principally into protection— protection of life, liberty, and property. Laws, wisely administered, will secure men in the enjoyment of the fruits of their labor, whether of mind or body, at a comparatively small personal sacrifice; but no laws, however stringent, can make the idle industrious, the thriftless provident, or the drunken sober. Such reforms can only be effected by means of individual action, economy, and self-denial; by better habits, rather than by greater rights.

The Government of a nation itself is usually found to be but the reflex of the individuals composing it. The Government that is ahead of the people will inevitably be dragged down to their level, as the Government that is behind them will in the long run be dragged up. In the order of nature, the collective character of a nation will as surely find its befitting results in its law and government, as water finds its own level. The noble people will be nobly ruled, and the ignorant and corrupt ignobly. Indeed, all experience serves to prove that the worth and strength of a State depend far less upon the form of its institutions than upon the character of its men. For the nation is only an aggregate of individual conditions, and civilization itself is but a question of the personal improvement of the men, women, and children of whom society is composed.

National progress is the sum of individual industry, energy, and uprightness, as national decay is of individual idleness, selfishness, and vice. What we are accustomed to decry as great social evils, will for the most part be found to be but the outgrowth of man's own perverted life; and though we may endeavor to cut them down and extirpate them by means of Law, they will only spring up again with fresh luxuriance in some other form, unless the conditions of personal life and character are radically improved. If this view be correct, then it follows that the highest patriotism and philanthropy consist, not so much in altering laws and modifying institutions, as in helping and stimulating men to elevate and improve themselves by their own free and independent individual action. . . . The solid foundations of liberty must rest upon individual character; which is also the only sure guaranty for social security and national progress. John Stuart Mill truly observes that "even despotism does not produce its worst effects so long as individuality exists under it; and whatever crushes individuality *is* despotism, by whatever name it be called."

* * *

The spirit of self-help, as exhibited in the energetic action of individuals, has in all times been a marked feature in the English character, and furnishes the true measure of our power as a nation. Rising above the heads of the mass, there were always to be found a series of individuals distinguished beyond others, who commanded the public homage. But our progress has also been owing to multitudes of smaller and less known men. Though only the generals' names may be remembered in the history of any great campaign, it has been in a great measure through the individual valor and heroism of the privates that victories have been won. And life, too, is "a soldier's battle"—men in the ranks having in all times been among the greatest of workers. Many are the lives of men unwritten, which have nevertheless as powerfully influenced civilization and progress as the more fortunate Great whose names are recorded in biography. Even the humblest person, who sets before his fellows an example of industry, sobriety, and upright honesty of purpose in life, has a present as well as a future influence upon the well-being of his country; for his life and character pass unconsciously into the lives of others, and propagate good example for all time to come.

Daily experience shows that it is energetic individualism which produces the most powerful effects upon the life and action of others, and really constitutes the best practical education. Schools, academies, and colleges give but the merest beginnings of culture in comparison with it. Far more influential is the life-education daily given in our homes, in the streets, behind counters, in work-shops, at the loom and the plow, in counting-houses and manufactories, and in the busy haunts of men.

*   *   *

Any class of men that lives from hand to mouth will ever be an inferior class. They will necessarily remain impotent and helpless, hanging on to the skirts of society, the sport of times and seasons. Having no respect for themselves, they will fail in securing the respect of others. In commercial crises, such men must inevitably go to the wall. Wanting that husbanded power which a store of savings, no matter how small, invariably gives them, they will be at every man's mercy, and, if possessed of right feelings, they cannot but regard with fear and trembling the future possible fate of their wives and children. "The world," once said Mr. Cobden to the workingmen of Huddersfield, "has always been divided into two classes—those who have saved, and those who have spent—the thrifty and the extravagant. The building of all the houses, the mills, the bridges, and the ships, and the accomplishment of all other great works which have rendered man civilized and happy, has been done by the savers, the thrifty; and those who have wasted their resources have always been their slaves. It has been the law of nature and of Providence that this should be so; and I were an imposter if I promised any class that they would advance themselves if they were improvident, thoughtless and idle."

Equally sound was the advice given by Mr. Bright to an assembly of workingmen at Rochdale, in 1847, when, after expressing his belief that, "so far as honesty was concerned, it was to be found in pretty equal amount among all classes," he used the following words: "There is only one way that is safe for any man or any number of men, by which they can maintain their present position if it be a good one, or raise themselves above it if it be a bad one—that is, by the practice of the virtues of industry, frugality, temperance and honesty. There is no royal road by which men can raise themselves from a position which they feel to be uncomfortable and unsatisfactory, as regards their mental or physical condition, except by the practice of those virtues by which they find numbers among them are continually advancing and bettering themselves."

Alan Bullock and Maurice Shock

THE MORAL IMPERATIVE OF LIBERALISM

What saved Victorian liberalism from the damning charge of indifference or callousness toward poverty and injustice was its moral dimension. Men like Gladstone (1809–1898), who himself was for thirty years the "conscience of England," put an indelible moral imprint on English liberalism. This passion for liberty and justice was the key to Gladstone's foreign and Irish policies. Was his claim that "liberty alone fits men for liberty" a sufficient answer to social problems? The following essay illuminates the moral imperative in Gladstonian liberalism. Its authors are two Oxford historians, Alan Bullock, Master of St. Catherine's College and Vice-Chancellor of Oxford University, and Maurice Shock, Fellow and Praelector in Politics of University College.

The liberalism of Mill's essay *On Liberty* . . . represents an emancipation from influences to which the Liberal tradition owed much of its strength but also a certain narrow-mindedness in its earlier phase. This emancipation finds its clearest expression in Gladstone.

For Gladstone, as J. L. Hammond points out, combined the religious feeling of a Wilberforce or a Shaftesbury with a passion for the classical civilisation of Greece and Rome. His Christianity was illuminated by his love of Homer and Aristotle, Augustine and Dante. These, together with Bishop Butler and Burke, were the influences which had the deepest effect on him and gave him an intellectual approach to Liberalism wholly different from that of a man like Bright [a radical Liberal colleague who led the anti-corn law agitation and popularized the egalitarian aspect of liberalism].

On one side of his complex personality Gladstone was an orthodox Liberal and it was this side which was uppermost in his career until his first retirement in 1874. Had Gladstone died then at the age of sixty-five he would have appeared as the man who had put into effect (as Chancellor of the Exchequer from 1859 to 1865 and as Prime Minister from 1868 to 1874) the programme of Liberal reforms which Cobden had once called on Peel, Gladstone's master, to carry out.

Free trade, a commercial treaty with France, the abolition of

From Alan Bullock and Maurice Shock, *The Liberal Tradition: From Fox to Keynes* (London: A. & C. Black, Ltd., 1956), pp. xxxvii–xli. Reprinted by permission of the publisher.

the paper duties, the reduction of expenditure and taxation, the dis-establishment of the Irish Church, the Education Act of 1870, the Ballot Act, the opening of the Universities to Nonconformists and of the Civil Service to competitive examination, Cardwell's Army reforms, the Alabama arbitration and neutrality in the Franco-Prus-sian War—it was an impressive record, but all well within the canon of accepted Liberal ideas.

Where Gladstone made his own individual contribution and en-larged the Liberal tradition was in the two crusades which brought him back into politics after 1874: foreign policy and the Irish question. On both issues his attitude gave expression to the vivid conception of the place of the moral law in the relations between nations which made him the most controversial figure of his age.

Gladstone's ideas on foreign policy were not those of Cobden and Bright. Far from advocating non-intervention, he insisted (for example, in the Eastern crisis of 1875–8) on England's duty to intervene and to pursue an active policy. Where he differed from Palmerston and Disraeli was on the grounds of intervention and the objectives of an active foreign policy.

Although there are many anticipations of his views on earlier occasions, they find their clearest expression in the sustained attack which he made on Disraeli's foreign policy in the 1870's and which reached its climax in the Midlothian campaign of 1879–80.

Gladstone took as his starting-point the principle that foreign policy ought to be conducted in accordance with the demands of justice, not of expediency or power. He condemned "a vigorous, that is to say, a narrow, restless, blustering and self-asserting for-eign policy . . . appealing to the selflove and pride of the com-munity" and setting up national interests selfishly conceived ("a new and base idolatry") as its sole objective. "I appeal to an established tradition, older, wiser, nobler far—a tradition not which disregards British interests, but which teaches you to seek the promotions of those interests in obeying the dictates of honour and of justice."

Throughout his life Gladstone felt a passionate sympathy for peoples struggling to achieve national independence. This provides the other foundation of his views on foreign policy. "The powers of self-government," this was his answer alike to the problems of the Balkans and those of Ireland. "Give those people freedom and the benefits of freedom," he said of Turkey's Christian subjects in 1880, "that is the way to make a barrier against despotism. Fortresses may be levelled to the ground; treaties may be trodden under foot—the true barrier against despotism is in the human heart and the human mind."

From this sympathy it followed for Gladstone that all nations should enjoy equality of rights. "To claim anything more than equality of rights in the moral and political intercourse of the world is not the way to make England great, but to make it both morally and materially little." From this in turn sprang his condemnation of imperialism which proclaimed supremacy, not equality, and in its eagerness for aggrandisement brushed aside the rights of other nations to bring them under alien rule.

Back in office after 1880, Gladstone failed to put these principles into practice. The occupation of Egypt accorded ill with the spirit of the Midlothian campaign and his views on foreign policy proved less and less applicable to the rivalries of the Great Powers as the 19th century drew to its close. But the ideas to which he gave currency, far from losing their hold upon the Liberal imagination, have gained in strength since 1914. In the hopes placed in the League of Nations and the United Nations, in the attempt to organise collective security and the disappointed but constantly renewed appeals to world opinion against injustice and aggression, in the demand of the peoples of Asia, Africa and the Middle East for self-government, Gladstone's beliefs have found a frustrated but passionate confirmation.

It was in his campaign for Irish Home Rule that Gladstone himself tried most tenaciously to carry out his ideas. He came to see the Irish question, not as a domestic problem of law and order—any more than the American question had been in the 1770's—but as the claim of a nation to self-government, as much deserving of sympathy as the claims of the Italians, the Greeks and the Bulgars. Gladstone's determination to satisfy this claim deeply affected the fortunes of Liberalism for years to come. It split the Liberal Party, put back the cause of social reform for a generation, necessitated a dangerous alliance with the Irish Nationalists, and, because of its unpopularity in England, was electorally disastrous. In spite of all this Gladstone and his followers were convinced that justice for

Ireland was the great culminating work of the Liberal tradition. Ireland was the touchstone of that sympathy which Liberal England had shown so generously in the case of others: was it now to be overridden by self-interest when it was a question of Britain's own empire?

Self-government had already been granted to Canada and the other colonies with the most felicitous results. No more was being asked for Ireland where, by contrast, "the first conditions of civil life—the free course of law, the liberty of every individual in the exercise of every legal right, the confidence of the people in the law and their sympathy with the law" were entirely absent. It was only in Ireland that the sovereign Liberal remedy of freedom had not been tried. Elsewhere it had never failed and the settlement of Ireland, the thorniest question in British politics, would be its supreme justification.

II LIBERALISM IN FLUX

Edward H. Carr
THE MORAL BANKRUPTCY OF LIBERALISM

Equal opportunity and fair and free competition were fundamental economic and moral assumptions of laissez-faire liberalism. Edward H. Carr (1892–), Fellow of Trinity College, Cambridge, and author of numerous international studies, including The Twenty Years' Crisis, 1919–1939 *and* A History of Russia, *challenges these assumptions. He claims that the competitors do not, in fact, start free and equal, and that the longer the competition continues, the more unequal the contest becomes. His thesis is drawn from the following observations.*

The new society was to be a society of free and equal individuals. The dictates of economic morality were henceforth summed up in obedience to the laws of the market; the individual pursuing his own economic interest was assumed to be promoting that of the whole society. Minor local and sectional loyalties were merged in the larger loyalty of the individual to his nation, of the citizen to the state. It was taken for granted that even this loyalty would soon be merged in a still larger loyalty to the whole community of mankind (which was the logical corollary of the single world market) and that the citizen of a single state or nation would be superseded by the citizen of the world.

The nineteenth-century economic society produced its own corresponding political order and political philosophy; and for a lucid and succinct summary of them one cannot do better than turn to Macaulay, that unrivalled expositor of the current ideas of his age:

> *Our rulers will best promote the improvement of the nation by strictly confining themselves to their own legitimate duties, by leaving capital to find its own most lucrative course, commodities their fair price, industry and intelligence their natural reward, idleness and folly their natural punishment, by maintaining peace, by defending property, by diminishing the price of law, and by observing strict economy in every department of the state. Let the government do this: the people will assuredly do the rest.*

From Edward H. Carr, *The New Society* (New York: St. Martin's Press, 1960), pp. 20–24, 26. Reprinted by permission of St. Martin's Press, Inc., The Macmillan Company of Canada, and Macmillan & Co., Ltd.

. . . In this society of free and equal individuals harmoniously competing against one another for the common good the state had no need to intervene. It did not intervene economically—to control production or trade, prices or wages; and still less politically—to guide and influence opinion. It held the ring to prevent foul play and to protect the rights of property against malefactors. Its functions were police functions. It was what Lassalle, the German socialist, contemptuously called the "night-watchman state."

There is no more fascinating theme in contemporary history than to follow the stages through which the *laissez-faire* "night-watchman state" of the nineteenth century has been transformed into the "welfare state" of today—at one and the same time its logical opposite and its logical corollary. The process was, of course, gradual and had begun long before the twentieth century or the first world war. While the industrial revolution was still in its infancy, Robert Owen had issued a warning against the danger of giving it its head and pleaded for state action to curb some of its consequences:

> *The general diffusion of manufactures throughout a country [he wrote in 1817] generates a new character in its inhabitants; and, as this character is formed on a principle quite unfavourable to individual or general happiness, it will produce the most lamentable and permanent evils unless its tendency be counteracted by legislative interference and direction.*

The humanitarian movements which led to extensive factory legislation to protect, at first the child worker and the woman worker, and later workers in general, against extreme forms of physical exploitation, were well under way in Britain in the 1840's.

Social pressures brought about these enactments in the most advanced and densely populated industrial countries before any widespread conscious departure from the *laissez-faire* philosophy could be discerned. But they were symptoms of a profound underlying refusal to accept the continued validity of that philosophy and of the presuppositions on which it rested. The conception of a society where success was, in Macaulay's terminology, the "natural reward" of "industry and intelligence," and failure the "natural punishment" of "idleness and folly," was not particularly humane. But it was clear-cut, logical and coherent on one hypothesis—

namely that the free and equal individuals who competed for these rewards and punishments did, in fact, start free and equal. What ultimately discredited the philosophy which Macaulay had so confidently enunciated was the realization that the competitors did not start free and equal and that, the longer the competition continued, the less scope was left for freedom and equality, so that the moral foundation on which *laissez-faire* rested was more and more hopelessly undermined. . . .

In Great Britain and in the chief European countries, the industrial revolution broke in on a long-standing traditional order based on social hierarchy. The economic and social inequalities left behind by the *ancien régime* made impossible anything like the clean start between the competitors which was assumed by the exponents of *laissez-faire.* But this flaw, much less in evidence in the new world of America than in old Europe, was not very important. What was far more serious was that the revolution, which purported to wipe out the old inequalities and did in large measure wipe them out, soon bred and tolerated new inequalities of its own. The notion of a society in which individuals start equal on equal terms in each generation—the unqualified recognition of *la carrière ouverte aux talents*—is soon tripped up by what seems to be a deep-seated human instinct. However firmly we may in theory believe in an equal start for everyone in the race, we have no desire that our children should start equal with the children of the Joneses—assuming that our greater wealth or more highly placed connexions enable us to give them the initial advantage of better nutrition, better medical care, better education or better opportunities of every kind.

. . . In every society, however egalitarian in principle, inherited advantages quickly set in motion the process of building up a ruling class, even if the new ruling class has not the additional asset of being able in part to build on the foundations of the old. And so it happened in the industrial society of the nineteenth century; and the story of the industrious errand-boy who became the managing director and of the lazy son of the managing director who became an errand-boy was soon an agreeable myth which took little or no account of the facts of life. But, when this myth was exploded, it carried away with it whatever moral justification had existed for the non-intervention of the state in a society where industry and intelligence were automatically rewarded and idleness and folly automatically punished.

Nor did the trouble stop there. What was much worse than any inequality of initial opportunity was the fact that individuals engaged in the economic process obstinately refused to remain individuals. Instead of competing against one another on equal terms for the good of all, they began to combine with one another in groups for their own exclusive profit.

*   *   *

This summary outline is enough to show that contemporary forms of economic organization, while they are in one sense a direct negation of the *laissez-faire* system, in another sense proceed directly from it. The result of free competition has been to destroy competition; competing individuals have replaced themselves by monopolistic groups as the economic units. The further, however, this process advances, the more untenable becomes the conception of non-interference by the state.

John Wesley Derry
MILL'S MODIFICATION OF LIBERALISM

Rigorously educated as a Benthamite liberal, John Stuart Mill (1806–1873) first responded to, and then revolted against, the rigidities of utilitarian thought. His honesty and social sensitivities forced an agonizing reappraisal of the inability of classical liberalism to cope with the inequities of industrial society. The evolution of Mill's views embodies the transformations that were occurring in English liberalism. The anxieties which made Mill an apologist for change, yet uneasy about the shape of those changes, are the focus of John Wesley Derry's interpretation. A Fellow of Downing College, Cambridge, and formerly a lecturer in political science at the London School of Economics, Derry observes in Mill the interplay of ideas and political and

From John Wesley Derry, *The Radical Tradition* (New York: St. Martin's Press, Inc., 1967), pp. 236–237, 247–248, 251–257, 266–267, 272–273. Reprinted by permission of St. Martin's Press, Inc., The Macmillan Company of Canada, and Macmillan & Co., Ltd.

social forces. Unlike earlier liberals, Mill sensed that free political institutions must be rooted in a liberal social environment in order to survive.

Ever since the age of Paine Radicalism had been a confident creed, bristling with certitude and never slow to castigate the privileged or corrupt. . . . The impact of industrialism and the frustrations of the post-war years did not weaken Radicalism's faith in itself. Cobbett, Owen, Place, and Hume never doubted their own wisdom or questioned their own insight. . . . Even the most intellectually aware of the Radicals—the Benthamites—were not men torn by doubt. They knew the secret of good, efficient, and cheap government and they did not shirk the responsibilities of applying their remedies, whenever the opportunity came to them.

But from the innermost citadel of Benthamism the most self-critical of the Utilitarians emerged to do self-conscious battle for the truth against established error and traditional folly. John Stuart Mill represented Radicalism at its most coherent and at its most anxious. Rigid to the point of being doctrinaire on some issues he nevertheless found himself perplexed by doubt. Haunted by a sense of personal inadequacy he was called to a high vocation as the apostle of the religion of humanity. Other Radicals, such as Paine and Owen, had allowed nothing—no experience of humiliation or defeat—to disturb the certainty of their basic philosophy, but Mill responded to new situations and to new moods with a sensitivity which led him to thrash about in tortured desperation for a way of reconciling an awareness of the complexity of life with the pristine simplicity of the old revelation. The saint of rationalism—to use Gladstone's generous phrase—knew the agonies of self-doubt, and the knowledge that he, above all men, was the guardian of the faith once revealed to Jeremy Bentham and expounded so pugnaciously by his father, weighed heavily upon his soul. Mill had seen enough of what Radicalism had achieved to be driven to question much of what it believed. Furthermore, he revealed in his own person the dilemma of Victorian Liberalism in its attitude to the growing power of government, to the challenge of democracy, and to the modern, industrialised state.

*　　*　　*

Dedicated as he was to justice and equality he was unhappy about the means by which these commendable blessings were to be attained. An all-powerful state would deprive men of liberty, imposing a dull mediocrity and an unquestioning orthodoxy upon mankind. The advocate of Parliamentary reform had misgivings about the nature of representation: How could society be protected from the domination of the ignorant? How could excellence be preserved in a society striving to achieve a real measure of equality? Mill longed for ways to give extra weight to the intelligent and educated sections in the community. He changed his mind on the merits of the secret ballot, seeing it as a danger to the responsible exercise of a privilege and a trust. As the years went by he became preoccupied with the place of minorities in the modern state. He attempted to lay down necessary limits on the scope of government. This was the germ of his most famous book—*On Liberty*. It was, in many ways, a classic defence of a traditional position. It was the repository for Mill's most anxious thoughts. . . .

Mill stated his purpose clearly:

> The object of this Essay is to assert one very simple principle, as entitled to govern absolutely the dealings of society with the individual in the way of compulsion and control, whether the means used be physical force in the form of legal penalties, or the moral coercion of public opinion. That principle is, that the sole end for which mankind are warranted, individually or collectively, in interfering with the liberty of action of any of their number is self-protection. That the only purpose for which power can be rightfully exercised over any member of a civilised community, against his will, is to prevent harm to others. His own good, either physical or moral, is not itself a sufficient warrant.

The individual was responsible to society only for that part of his conduct which concerned others. Over his own mind and body he was sovereign.

This was Mill's response to what he believed to be the great evil of his time: the increasing inclination to extend the powers of the state, both through opinion and legislation. The threat to the free and spontaneous development of the individual was all the more grave because far from disappearing in the course of time it was becoming all the more formidable. It was important, therefore, for men to recognise the sphere in which society, as distinguished from the individual, had, at best, only an indirect interest.

* * *

He affirmed his belief in free speech because he was worried that in an industrialised democracy it would be threatened, not by government legislation, but by the prejudices and passions of the uneducated masses. Freedom of opinion was the only security against tyranny of opinion, the surest means of defending the enlightened minority from the social pressure to conform.

Freedom of choice was also fundamental. Perception, judgment, and discrimination were the fruits of choosing. It was as enervating to do what the majority did, simply because it was the majority, as it was stultifying to think what the majority thought for the same reason. Conformity imposed from without was fatal to the inward forces which Mill believed to be the essential elements in the growth of the mature personality. Conformism was more deplorable because it was enforced by social convention.

> *In our times, from the highest class of society down to the lowest, every one lives as under the eye of a hostile and dreaded censorship. Not only in what concerns others, but in what concerns only themselves, the individual or the family do not ask themselves—what do I prefer? or, what would suit my character and disposition? . . . They ask themselves, what is suitable to my position? what is usually done by persons of my station? . . . or (worse still) what is usually done by persons of a station and circumstances superior to mine? . . . It does not occur to them to have any inclination, except for what is customary. Thus, the mind itself is bowed to the yoke. . . .*

Instead of a rich individuality, social convention encouraged the prevalence of a dull mediocrity. Men shrank from the unconventional, suppressing their own inclinations because of the need to conform. Instead of relying on their own insight men preferred to accept the placid generalities of conventional belief. Acceptability was valued more highly than perception. Yet the progress of the human race could spring only from the full development of the individual. Society could be enriched only if its members were encouraged to develop their aptitudes to the full, without subjecting originality of mind to the censorship of convention. In proportion to the development of his individuality each person became more valuable to himself and to society. "It is," Mill argued, "only the cultivation of individuality which produces, or can produce, well-developed human beings."

Conscious of the charge that liberalism was preoccupied with the individual, to the detriment of the community, Mill affirmed that though doctrines of social contract were fictitious, every one who received the protection of society owed a return for this benefit. Every one was responsible for his conduct towards other members of society. The first social obligation was to abstain from injuring others; the second was the acceptance of the duty to defend others from injury or molestation. Nor were all injuries of the sort that called for legal action: in some instances the offender could rightly be punished by opinion rather than by law.

But because Mill accepted the legitimate role of opinion (even, so far as the offending individual was concerned, tyrannous opinion) in disciplining the community, he sought to insure the individual against unfair persecution by laying down the general principle which was to govern society's attitude towards the behaviour of its members. All that Mill could resort to here was to make a distinction between self-regarding actions, which did not affect other members of the community; and other-regarding actions, which adversely impinged upon those who, whether they wished it or not, were affected by the actions of their fellow-citizens. If a person disabled himself, even by conduct which at first seemed essentially self-regarding, from the performance of duties which had been laid upon him by the community, then he had committed a social offence. "No person ought to be punished simply for being drunk; but a soldier or a policeman should be punished for being drunk on duty. Whenever, in short, there is a definite damage, or a definite risk of damage, either to an individual or to the public, the case is taken out of the province of liberty, and placed in that of morality or law."

Mill's distinction was much less satisfactory than he believed. It was more convincing in theory than in practice. There are few actions which can be said to be wholly self-regarding, and what Mill propounded as a valid legislative and social principle was little more than a handy—but rough and ready—rule of thumb. The issue was further complicated by the fact that there may be cases in which intervention by the community is, theoretically at least, desirable for the well-being of various members of society but where such intervention is impracticable: the law may therefore be evaded or defied with impunity. There are other areas of conduct in which attempts to reward acceptable behaviour and penalise undesirable behaviour can work only in an arbitrary and unfair manner, bringing both the law and convention into ill repute. There are other types of behaviour about which it is impossible to reach agreement as to whether or not the interference of society is justifiable. Mill was primarily concerned with defending the unconventional individual from undue interference, and if taken seriously his principle was more convincing as a negative insurance against inquisition than as a valid rule for social control.

In any case, Mill harboured a strong prejudice against governmental intervention. Governments tended to interfere in the wrong place and in the wrong ways. This was especially true in the sphere of personal conduct. Even when he was prepared to concede that the majority might be right about social morality (other-regarding actions) he argued that they would almost certainly be wrong on questions of private morality (self-regarding actions). Even when it provided positive services for the community, government was to be viewed suspiciously. To rely upon the government whenever the aim contemplated could be better achieved by individuals was patently foolish. Even when government action was likely to be more efficient this did not necessarily justify governmental initiative. There were cases in which individuals would benefit from exercising their faculties and their judgment, learning from their mistakes and enjoying the privilege of participating in the running of affairs, rather than submitting to the tyranny of the expert which was scarcely less objectionable than the tyranny of the ignorant. The more a government interfered in the way in which society was organised the greater would its power be. This would reduce an ever greater portion of the community to the status of abject hangers-on, the passive recipients of governmental or party charity. Initiative and vitality would be sapped, and the enlightened individual would be more dangerously exposed to conformist pressures. Most deplorable of all, if the government became the biggest agent of social activity, it would attract a disproportionate amount of talent into its ranks, depriving other aspects of community life of intelligence and vigour. "The worth of a State, in the long run, is the worth of the individuals composing it; and a State which postpones the interests of their mental expansion and elevation to a little more of administrative skill . . . will find that with small men no great thing can really be accomplished."

Whenever Mill admitted that some degree of state intervention was called for he did so with extreme caution. Education was an instance in which his desire to educate the masses conflicted with his hesitancy about the means by which this was to be accomplished. His dislike of sectarian educational establishments drew him inexorably towards secular education organised by the state; but he was reluctant to permit the state to direct or control education. He feared that indoctrination, rather than the free development of the individual, would be the inevitable consequence. . . .

His misgivings over the increasing role of the state were paralleled by his anxiety over the approach of democracy. Just as he feared that the outstanding individual would be crushed by the mediocre mass in the realm of ideas and ethics, so he feared that democracy would corrupt public life and install the rule of the ignorant. The chief purpose of government was the promotion of the virtue and intelligence of the people: political institutions were to be assessed according to the extent to which they fostered the moral and intellectual qualities in the life of the community. There was no indefinable magic about forms of government. They did not spring up overnight. They were the work of men, and if they were to function properly they needed careful scrutiny. Most important of all, they needed the active participation of the people themselves.

. . . Ideally the individual citizen ought to share, not merely in the sovereignty of the people, but also in the functions of government by the personal discharge of some of its duties. It was this element of participation which Mill felt to be threatened by the mass democracy which he saw emerging. He believed in democracy, in so far as he thought that the people were ultimately sovereign. But he was acutely conscious of the immediate dangers to the qualities of excellence which he so admired: the swamping of judgment by the crude power of numbers, the decline of politics to the level of the mass corruption of the electorate, the neglect of intellect and the triumph of class legislation. He believed that as long as the masses were ignorant they would be exploited by those who did not have the true interests of the country at heart. And so, for all his faith in representative government and his sympathy for democracy as an ideal, he recognised and deplored the dangers implicit in the mid-nineteenth-century situation. These dangers could be reduced to two heads: "First, general ignorance and incapacity, or, to speak more moderately, insufficient mental qualifications, in the controlling body; secondly, the danger of its being under the influence of interests not identical with the general welfare of the community."

The most serious problem facing those who believed in representative forms of government was how to provide securities against these evils, and, more especially, how to protect those minorities upon whom the future vitality of the community depended. The natural tendency of modern civilisation was, in Mill's view, a tendency towards collective mediocrity. It was heightened by those extensions of the franchise which were put forward as the means by which democracy was to be inaugurated. It was essential, therefore, that any extension of the franchise should be accompanied by some increased representation for education and intellect. . . .

Mill believed that no one who was illiterate or who was incapable of doing a simple arithmetic sum should be allowed to vote. Once adequate educational opportunities were provided for all this would be a fair test of the elector's fitness for the franchise. If there were any clash between the two priorities Mill did not hesitate: "universal teaching must precede universal enfranchisement."

Nor was he happy with the idea that those who paid no taxes should have the dominant voice in public affairs. This would remove the usual incentives toward economy: the temptation to be lavish or extravagant with other people's money was one which ought not to arise in a civilised community. He remembered the traditional association between representation and taxation. The best method of preserving this link was to ensure that taxation—"in a visible shape" —should descend to the poorest class. One way of doing this would be to insist that every elector should pay a small annual sum to the exchequer. Nor did Mill like the prospect of those who were in receipt of poor relief getting the vote: those who could not support themselves had no right to help themselves to the money of others. None of these restrictions excluded a class of citizens from the privileges of the suffrage, but they ensured that those who participated in the choosing of representatives should have some status in the community and some degree of responsibility.

But while Mill was willing to debar those who failed to reach minimal standards for the exercise of the vote, he was more interested in giving additional electoral weight to the more intelligent and better educated members of society. In this way democracy would function without prejudice to the enlightened minority, while the quality of public life would be maintained.

*   *   *

His own experience had demonstrated the deficiencies of Utilitarianism (which he admitted) and of rationalism (which, perhaps because of Harriet,[1] he never dared fully to admit). Mill has often been portrayed as an honest seeker after truth, a saint born out of his time, a man of religious susceptibilities tormented by the difficulties of a secular and scientific age. But it is nearer the truth to see him as a dogmatic rationalist, perplexed by doubts which rationalism could never quell, who yet lacked the confidence to yield fully to the promptings of his feelings. He was more sensitive to certain types of emotion than he ought to have been, assuming that he wished to preserve his rationalist faith intact. Lacking both the open-mindedness which he so admired, and the confidence of the pious believer who knew no doubt, Mill wandered uneasily in the no man's land of sensitive scepticism. He never fully avowed his misgivings, and whatever the complexities of his emotional life, intellectually he clung, with some difficulty, to the dogmas of reason and duty.

The same confusion is evident in his attitude towards the state, society, and government. It is not wholly convincing to say that he was devoid of any appreciation of society, and the individualism of *On Liberty* has obscured his concern for the creation of a society in which culture and enlightenment (as he understood them) were propagated by the new clerisy, the rationalist intelligentsia. His

[1] Harriet (Hardy) Taylor, who became his wife in 1851. Mill claimed that she was his superior both as a poet and as a thinker.—Ed.

defence of the rights of the individual was a defensive response to the tendencies which he detected in mid-Victorian England towards mass urban democracy, without the necessary prerequisite of a national system of education. Similarly, the doubts which he eventually expressed about such specimens of Radical piety as the secret ballot and manhood suffrage were the outcome of an emotional revulsion from the consequences, in practice or in prospect, of those assumptions which he had accepted so idealistically in his younger days. On no level did he fuse his experience of life and his emotional development with a coherent rethinking of his intellectual position. In this, as in much else, he was a representative Victorian.

Society could be accepted as the sphere in which the individual fulfilled himself or as the realm over which the new clerisy presided with perception and authority. But Mill never evolved a convincing justification for the state as a positive agency for the good life. His concessions were fragmentary and inconsistent. Too often he fell back on the reiteration of pious phrases, not to express ideas but to cloak them in the comforting robes of ambiguity. He urged the primary value of spontaneity in the development of the individual, but he was content to see the state and society as enemies, rather than the agents, of free choice. T. H. Green adapted Hegelian idealism to English conditions, justifying the state on idealistic grounds yet attempting to ensure the virtues of choice, spontaneity, and participation. Mill never achieved anything as impressive or as coherent. He flattered himself that he followed the truth wherever it led, that he always thought an idea through to its ultimate conclusion. In fact he rarely accomplished this. Had he examined the assumptions which determined his thought he might well have resolved some of the doubts and difficulties which persistently tormented him.

*   *   *

When Mill died on 7 May 1873 he was content. He believed that his work was complete. Much remained to be done, but as a writer and a theorist he had blazed a trail and that was itself enough.

His place in the history of English Radicalism is perplexing. So often he epitomised all that advanced opinion demanded: Parliamentary reform, the ballot, the abolition of religious privileges, the emancipation of women, the establishment of democracy, the spread of education. Yet on all of these subjects—with the exception of the emancipation of women—Mill constantly gave way to doubts and misgivings. Even the Religion of Humanity was found wanting, though it was never formally abandoned. As he approached the realisation of his visions Mill stepped back from reality. As a man who was both authoritarian and liberal he was able to preserve his equilibrium only in the realm of speculation. An advance in theory was often succeeded by a retreat in practice. As a propagandist he strove to convince men of the efficacy of his ideas, seeking to make them more attractive and compelling. If a rational establishment was eventually to be substituted for a Christian one it was to be accomplished by persuasion not by force. But Mill became more aware of the limitations of his own outlook, however lacking he was in the tenacity or the power to transcend them. So it came about that the apologist for change was ill at ease in a changing world, reflecting in his own person the confidence and the anxiety which lay at the root of so much of the tension and tribulation of mid-Victorian society. With Mill English Radicalism ate of the forbidden fruit of the tree of knowledge: with him the age of innocence is past.

Robert Lowe

DANGERS OF DEMOCRACY FOR LIBERALISM

"He cannot help being brilliant," wrote Walter Bagehot of his contemporary, Robert Lowe (1811–1892). A Liberal member of Parliament and writer for the Times *endowed with a keen, first-class mind, Lowe led the Whig opposition to Lord Russell's Reform Bill in 1866 and brought about its defeat. But his arguments were swept aside the next year by the tide of democracy. Lowe's fears of democracy were based largely on the conviction that government should be in the hands of an intelligent—and therefore limited—electorate. The following passage became the swan song of Lowe's version*

From Robert Lowe, *Speeches and Letters on Reform* (London: Robert J. Bush, 1867), pp. 4–9, 10–11, 15.

of middle-class liberalism: a society governed by propertied and talented electors who won the right to vote by raising their station instead of by lowering the standards of enfranchisement. His failure in 1867 to prevent the extension of the franchise, however, did not prevent him from accepting office the next year as chancellor of the exchequer in Gladstone's cabinet.

When I find a book or a speech appealing to abstract *a priori* principles I put it aside in despair, being well aware that I can learn nothing useful from it. Such works only present to us the limited and qualified propositions which experience has established, without their limitations and qualifications, and elevate them into principles by a rash generalization which strips them of whatever truth they originally possessed. Thus the words *right* and *equality* have a perfectly clear and defined meaning when applied to the administration of justice under a settled law, but are really without meaning, except as vague and inappropriate metaphors, when applied to the distribution of political power. The proper answer to a statement, for instance, that all men free from crime or pauperism have a right to the franchise, is—that this is a question of experience, not of *a priori* assumption, and that the assertion, whether true or false, is inadmissible in political discussion. But how is this truth to be made evident to a large multitude when we find men from whom better things might have been expected, speaking of those who deny the existence of rights as if they sought to deprive men of something they really possess, instead of to explode a vague and meaningless assumption? The position may be further illustrated by observing, that if the propositions of this nature which we hear were true, they would not lead, as they do, to false conclusions, such as —that men, women, and children, should have the franchise; that this right applies to every race in the world; that this right being prior to and independent of experience cannot be limited by experience, and that it is therefore the duty of a State to do what may be foreseen to lead to immediate ruin in order to satisfy these abstract principles which it has imposed on itself as its guide. The first step, therefore, in the discussion of democratic changes is to clear the mind of these delusive notions, and to employ the teaching of experience, not to qualify or limit, but absolutely to supersede them. . . .

What, then, is the professed object of Reform? It is to improve the structure of the House of Commons. The natural order of investigation is—What are the faults which require correction, and then how will the proposed measures cure those faults? Passion or party spirit may drive men to plunge into the details of a Reform Bill without clearly putting to themselves and answering these questions, but no really conscientious investigator can pass them by unconsidered.

. . . It is not for the evils that exist, but for the evils which it is in its power to prevent, that Parliament should be held responsible. Everybody admits this when he judges another in private life, but when we are dealing with public bodies, we cast candour aside, and censure them for things over which they have no control, or which they have done very wisely to let alone. The theory of uneducated or half-educated persons in general is, that Government is almost omnipotent, and that when an evil is not remedied the fault lies in the indolence, the selfishness, or the shortsightedness of Parliament. It is much pleasanter to an audience of non-electors to be told that the franchise would enable them to remedy the evils of their condition than to be told the real truth, that the evils they endure are remediable by themselves, in their individual rather than in their collective capacity—by their own thrift and self-denial, not by pressing on Government to do that for them which they are able, if they will, to do without it. It were ludicrous, if it were not so sad, to hear speeches which urge working-men to seek for the franchise, that they may compel Parliament to compel them to educate their children, or to practise an involuntary abstinence from intoxicating liquors. When one man is willing to sell his vote and another to buy it, what machinery does Parliament possess to prevent a secret bargain for its purchase? The Ballot nowhere secures secrecy, and the elections of America show that in large constituencies bribery is used as well as in small, especially when parties are evenly divided. Till Parliament can give health, strength, providence, and self-control, how can it deal with the evil of pauperism? If the poor were willing to pay a rent sufficient to provide them with decent and healthy dwellings, capital would flow into the business just as it does into the business of building public-houses and gin-shops. With what justice can Parliament be called upon to tax the community at large for that which it is in the power of all who receive fair wages to provide for themselves? These may suffice as specimens of the complaints of neglect of the interests of the poor which are brought against Parliament. Parliament does not command boundless resources. A course of the kind indicated would be felt very sensibly in heavier taxation, and a violation of sound principles would avenge itself on the very classes for whose supposed interest they were violated. . . .

The attempts to enlarge the sphere of Government action, which the impatience of benevolent persons urges upon us, can only be made at a heavy sacrifice of individual liberty. It is said Parliament should remedy the unequal distribution of land. This can only be done by curtailing individual liberty of disposition. That it should give compensation for improvements to tenants, this can only be done by invading the freedom of contract. Is it not at least conceivable that a Legislature which declines to enter on this retrograde course may be in the right, and actuated by better motives than prejudice in favour of one class or antipathy to another?

For my own part, I disclaim such motives. The end of good government appears to me to be the good of all, and, if that be not attainable, the good of the majority: but I must pause when I am told that the majority, told by the head, should have the supreme power because they will be sure to do that which is for their own interest. If this be so, the solution of all questions is easy indeed. Let us burn our books, and send round the ballot-box on every question as it arises? No position can be more unsound.

*　　*　　*

The more complicated and artificial society becomes, and the better we know the principles which underlie all sound legislation, the more difficult do we find it to do things which to our ancestors, three hundred years ago, presented no difficulty at all. Protection, for instance, is the political economy of the poor, simply because they are not able to follow the chain of reasoning which demonstrates that they themselves are sure to be the victims of the waste of capital which protection implies. I dare say that a democratic House of Commons would deal with many of these questions, especially those relating to protection, to the distribution of wealth, and the giving direct assistance to the poor from the public purse; but that does not prove that they would, by doing so, benefit the poor, or that the interest of the poor would be promoted by placing in their hands a more extended power of injuring themselves. From these considerations, it follows that, of those things which Parliament is blamed for not doing, many are impossible, others inexpedient, while some, such as the regulation of sanitary matters, have actually been attained without our censors being aware of it; that what is wanted is not more power to urge on change, but more intelligence to decide on what that change ought to be, and therefore that the standard of intelligence, in constituencies or members, should on no account be lowered, nor the impulse to inconsiderate action increased.

. . . But I would point out that the working classes, under the modest claim to share in electoral power, are really asking for the whole of it. Their claim is to pass from the position of non-electors to the position of sovereign arbiters in the last resort of the destinies of the nation. They who set up such a claim must show that they are masters of themselves before they can hope to be masters of others.

*   *   *

If it is competent to me to argue that with a little self-denial the franchise is already within the reach of many of them; that they will swamp the less numerous classes; that the expenses of elections will be increased, and the character of the House of Commons impaired; it is also competent for me to urge that since corruption and the other electoral vices prevail most in the lower ranks of the present constituencies, it is unwise and unsafe to go lower in search of electoral virtue.

Matthew Arnold
VULGARITY OF MIDDLE-CLASS LIBERALISM

Matthew Arnold (1822–1888) was one of the mid-century's most polished literary critics and poets. Son of Thomas Arnold, the famous headmaster of Rugby, he became professor of poetry at Oxford in 1857. His literary works centered on the role of culture in society. The questions Arnold raised inevitably led him to the consideration of politics. The human spirit, he wrote, was threatened by the anarchic conditions in English society. He attacked middle-class liberalism's fascination with progress and political machinery, advocating, instead, an authority of culture that would transcend class tensions and provide rule by "sweetness and light." Was such an authority possible, short of an absolute monarchy or a Platonic state? His ideas and his indictments of middle-class philistinism, set forth in Culture and Anarchy *(1869), were attacked from all sides—and continue to provoke controversy.*

But what was it, this Liberalism, as Dr. Newman [Oxford don and co-founder of the Oxford Movement who had become a cardinal in the Roman Catholic church] saw it, and as it really broke the Oxford movement? It was the great middle-class Liberalism, which had for the cardinal points of its belief the Reform Bill of 1832, and local self-government, in politics; in the social sphere, free-trade, unrestricted competition, and the making of large industrial fortunes; in the religious sphere, the Dissidence of Dissent and the Protestantism of the Protestant religion. I do not say that other and more intelligent forces than this were not opposed to the Oxford movement: but this was the force which really beat it; this was the force which Dr. Newman felt himself fighting with; this was the force which till only the other day seemed to be the paramount force in this country, and to be in possession of the future; this was the force whose achievements fill Mr. [Robert] Lowe with such inexpressible admiration, and whose rule he was so horror-struck to see threatened. And where is this great force of Philistinism now? It is thrust into the second rank, it is become a power of yesterday, it has lost the future. A new power has suddenly appeared, a power which it is impossible yet to judge fully, but which is certainly a wholly different

From Matthew Arnold, *Culture and Anarchy*, ed. with introd. J. Dover Wilson (New York: Cambridge University Press, 1960), pp. 62–65, 82, 88, 186–187, 204, 207. Reprinted by permission of Cambridge University Press.

force from middle-class Liberalism; different in its cardinal points of belief, different in its tendencies in every sphere. It loves and admires neither the legislation of middle-class Parliaments, nor the local self-government of middle-class vestries, nor the unrestricted competition of middle-class industrialists, nor the dissidence of middle-class Dissent and the Protestantism of middle-class Protestant religion. I am not now praising this new force, or saying that its own ideals are better; all I say is, that they are wholly different. And who will estimate how much the currents of feeling created by Dr. Newman's [Oxford] movement, the keen desire for beauty and sweetness which it nourished, the deep aversion it manifested to the hardness and vulgarity of middle-class Liberalism, the strong light it turned on the hideous and grotesque illusions of middle-class Protestantism—who will estimate how much all these contributed to swell the tide of secret dissatisfaction which has mined the ground under the self-confident Liberalism of the last thirty years, and has prepared the way for its sudden collapse and supersession? . . .

I have said that the new and more democratic force which is now superseding our old middle-class Liberalism cannot yet be rightly judged. It has its main tendencies still to form. We hear promises of its giving us administrative reform, law reform, reform of education, and I know not what; but those promises come rather from its advocates, wishing to make a good plea for it and to justify it for superseding middle-class Liberalism, than from clear tendencies which it has itself yet developed. But meanwhile it has plenty of well-intentioned friends against whom culture may with advantage continue to uphold steadily its ideal of human perfection; that this is *an inward spiritual activity, having for its characters increased sweetness, increased light, increased life, increased sympathy.* Mr. Bright [radical Liberal member of Parliament], who has a foot in both worlds, the world of middle-class Liberalism and the world of democracy, but who brings most of his ideas from the world of middle-class Liberalism in which he was bred, always inclines to inculcate that faith in machinery to which, as we have seen, Englishmen are so prone, and which has been the bane of middle-class Liberalism. He complains with a sorrowful indignation of people who "appear to have no proper estimate of the value of the franchise"; he leads his disciples to believe,—what the Englishman is always too ready to believe,—that the having a vote, like the having a large family, or a large business, or large muscles, has in itself some edifying and perfecting effect upon human nature.

. . . Why, this is just the very style of laudation with which Mr. Roebuck [an independent radical member of Parliament popular with the masses] or Mr. Lowe debauch the minds of the middle classes, and make such Philistines of them. It is the same fashion of teaching a man to value himself not on what he *is,* not on his progress in sweetness and light, but on the number of the railroads he has constructed, or the bigness of the tabernacle he has built. Only the middle classes are told they have done it all with their energy, self-reliance, and capital, and the democracy are told they have done it all with their hands and sinews. But teaching the democracy to put its trust in achievements of this kind is merely training them to be Philistines to take the place of the Philistines whom they are superseding; and they too, like the middle class, will be encouraged to sit down at the banquet of the future without having on a wedding garment, and nothing excellent can then come from them.

*   *   *

We have got a much wanted principle, a principle of authority, to counteract the tendency to anarchy which seems to be threatening us.

But how to organise this authority, or to what hands to entrust the wielding of it? How to get your *State,* summing up the right reason of the community, and giving effect to it, as circumstances may require, with vigour? And here I think I see my enemies waiting for me with a hungry joy in their eyes. But I shall elude them.

The *State,* the power most representing the right reason of the nation, and most worthy, therefore, of ruling,—of exercising, when circumstances require it, authority over us all,—is for Mr. Carlyle the aristocracy. For Mr. Lowe, it is the middle class with its incomparable Parliament. For the Reform League, it is the working class, the class with "the brightest powers of sympathy and readiest powers of action." Now, culture, with its disinterested pursuit of perfection, culture, simply trying to see things as they are, in order

to seize on the best and to make it prevail, is surely well fitted
to help us to judge rightly.

*   *   *

We have already seen how these things,—trade, business, and
population,—are mechanically pursued by us as ends precious in
themselves, and are worshipped as what we call fetishes; and Mr.
Bright, I have already said, when he wishes to give the working
class a true sense of what makes glory and greatness, tells it to look
at the cities it has built, the railroads it has made, the manufactures
it has produced. So to this idea of glory and greatness the free-trade
which our Liberal friends extol so solemnly and devoutly has served,
—to the increase of trade, business, and population; and for this it
is prized. Therefore, the untaxing of the poor man's bread has, with
this view of national happiness, been used not so much to make the
existing poor man's bread cheaper or more abundant, but rather to
create more poor men to eat it; so that we cannot precisely say that
we have fewer poor men than we had before free-trade, but we
can say with truth that we have many more centres of industry, as
they are called, and much more business, population, and manufactures. And if we are sometimes a little troubled by our multitude of
poor men, yet we know the increase of manufactures and population
to be such a salutary thing in itself, and our free-trade policy begets
such an admirable movement, creating fresh centres of industry and
fresh poor men here, while we were thinking about our poor men
there, that we are quite dazzled and borne away, and more and more
industrial movement is called for, and our social progress seems to
become one triumphant and enjoyable course of what is sometimes
called, vulgarly, outrunning the constable.

If, however, taking some other criterion of man's well-being than
the cities he has built and the manufactures he has produced, we
persist in thinking that our social progress would be happier if there
were not so many of us so very poor, and in busying ourselves with
notions of in some way or other adjusting the poor man and
business one to the other, and not multiplying the one and the other
mechanically and blindly, then our Liberal friends, the appointed
doctors of free-trade, take us up very sharply. "Art is long," says
the *Times,* "and life is short; for the most part we settle things first

and understand them afterwards. Let us have as few theories as possible; what is wanted is not the light of speculation. If nothing worked well of which the theory was not perfectly understood, we should be in sad confusion. The relations of labour and capital, we are told, are not understood, yet trade and commerce, on the whole, work satisfactorily."

*   *   *

Now I know, when I object that all this is machinery, the great Liberal middle class has by this time grown cunning enough to answer that it always meant more by these things than meets the eye; that it has had that within which passes show, and that we are soon going to see, in a Free Church and all manner of good things, what it was. But I have learned from Bishop Wilson (if Mr. Frederic Harrison will forgive my again quoting that poor old hierophant of a decayed superstition): "If we would really know our heart let us impartially view our actions"; and I cannot help thinking that if our Liberals had had so much sweetness and light in their inner minds as they allege, more of it must have come out in their sayings and doings.

*   *   *

Thus, in our eyes, the very framework and exterior order of the State, whoever may administer the State, is sacred; and culture is the most resolute enemy of anarchy, because of the great hopes and designs for the State which culture teaches us to nourish. But as, believing in right reason, and having faith in the progress of humanity towards perfection, and ever labouring for this end, we grow to have clearer sight of the ideas of right reason, and of the elements and helps of perfection, and come gradually to fill the framework of the State with them, to fashion its internal composition and all its laws and institutions conformably to them, and to make the State more and more the expression, as we say, of our best self, which is not manifold, and vulgar, and unstable, and contentious, and ever-varying, but one, and noble, and secure, and peaceful, and the same for all mankind,—with what aversion shall we not *then* regard anarchy, with what firmness shall we not check it, when there is so much that is so precious which it will endanger!

So that, for the sake of the present, but far more for the sake of the future, the lovers of culture are unswervingly and with a good conscience the opposers of anarchy. And not as the Barbarians and Philistines, whose honesty and whose sense of humour make them shrink, as we have seen, from treating the State as too serious a thing, and from giving it too much power;—for indeed the only State they know of, and think they administer, is the expression of their ordinary self.

*   *   *

Therefore, however great the changes to be accomplished, and however dense the array of Barbarians [aristocrats], Philistines [the middle class], and Populace [the masses], we will neither despair on the one hand, nor, on the other, threaten violent revolution and change. But we will look forward cheerfully and hopefully to "a revolution," as the Duke of Wellington said, "by due course of law"; though not exactly such laws as our Liberal friends are now, with their actual lights, fond of offering to us.[1]

---

[1] Arnold never spelled out what type of government his "authority of culture" demanded, but his sympathies, like those of Carlyle, seem to have run in favor of an authoritarianism that could curb the anarchistic forces he observed in English society. Sir Ernest Barker notes, "In the name of good taste or right reason he seeks an authority which will not pander to the bad taste of any class, and which must therefore, presumably, be non-representative; and it is difficult to see where such an authority can be found except in a sort of absolute monarchy. Arnold would have instantly denied that he sought anything of this order; he would have treated the idea with elusive and delicate irony; and yet this is the one logical issue of his teaching." *Political Thought in England, 1848 to 1914,* 2nd ed. (Oxford: Clarendon Press, 1928), p. 175. Cited by permission of the Clarendon Press, Oxford. —Ed.

John F. Glaser
DECLINE OF NONCONFORMIST CONSCIENCE

Nonconformity—the Protestant groupings outside the Church of England—identified readily with liberalism and provided it with much of its moral passion and dynamism. Did this alliance mean that liberalism and Nonconformity were so inseparable that the fortunes of liberalism were linked to the future of Nonconformity? This direct correlation is made in the article of John F. Glaser, professor of history at Ripon College, Wisconsin, and a specialist in the politics of nineteenth-century British Nonconformity. His treatment of Nonconformity should be compared with that offered by Matthew Arnold in the preceding selection.

By 1914 the Liberalism which had been the animating force of Victorian England and which experienced a vigorous renascence in Edwardian England seemed to have spent itself, unable to cope with the problems besetting Britain on the eve of the First World War. An essential part of the greatness and decline of Liberalism was the greatness and decline of English Nonconformity—the Protestant sects dissenting from the Church of England.[1] During the nineteenth century Nonconformists had been characterized by religious vitality and political strength, forming what Gladstone called "the backbone of British Liberalism." Seemingly more powerful than ever before at the beginning of the twentieth century, they contributed to and shared in the Liberal party triumph of 1906. Yet by 1914 it was apparent that Nonconformity, like Liberalism, had faltered; by the 1920's its religious vitality had markedly weakened and its political influence was negligible. It is the purpose of this article to examine

From John F. Glaser, "English Nonconformity and the Decline of Liberalism, *American Historical Review,* Vol. LXIII, No. 2, (1958), pp. 352–363. Reprinted by permission of the author.

[1] English Nonconformity embraces a wide theological spectrum, including Congregationalists, Baptists, Methodists, Presbyterians, Quakers, and Unitarians. In this article I shall follow the customary practice of using the collective terms "Nonconformity," "Dissent," and "Free Churches" interchangeably to designate all the Protestant groups outside of the Church of England. "Dissent," the standard term in the eighteenth century had become somewhat old-fashioned by the middle nineteenth century, when it was superseded by "Nonconformity" in popular usage. The modern Nonconformist preference for "Free Churches" may be dated officially from the formation of the National Free Church Council in 1892.

the crisis of English Liberalism in terms of the crisis of the Nonconformist conscience. The theme is significant because Liberalism—whether regarded as a political party, an economic creed, or a frame of mind—throughout its history was closely related to Nonconformity, from which it drew constant spiritual nourishment and material strength.

The term "Nonconformist conscience" first came into popular usage as a by-product of the Parnell affair in 1890. It was largely owing to Nonconformist pressure that Gladstone repudiated Parnell, a convicted adulterer and perjurer, and thus ensured his fall as leader of the Irish Parliamentary party. As the Methodist preacher Hugh Price Hughes thundered: "We stand immovably on this eternal rock; what is morally wrong can never be politically right." Though the Nonconformist conscience became best known as the custodian of a censorious personal morality, it stood for much more than that narrow aspect of Puritanism; it was the "insistence upon the authority of moral principle in all matters of public policy." In the broadest sense, the Nonconformist conscience embraced the whole of the Nonconformist political outlook.

In the nineteenth century this outlook was conditioned by three factors: the strict moral code and humanitarian zeal inculcated by Evangelicalism, the bitter sense of grievance engendered by the civil disabilities and social discrimination suffered by Dissenters, and the middle-class character of Nonconformity. The division between "church" and "chapel" cut deep into the everyday life of Victorian England, so that Nonconformists "grew up in the centre of the national life a separate and peculiar people." Yet the Evangelical revival had made these chapel-folk strong in numbers and energy, and they belonged predominantly to that middle class which was rising to economic power with the industrial revolution and to political power with the changes following the Reform Act of 1832. "Political Dissent," the movement for religious equality, had as its natural ally the individualistic Liberalism of the Manchester School. Attacking landed and Anglican Conservatism, the agitations for free trade and free church went hand in hand.

Both Nonconformity and Radicalism found their strength in the commercial and industrial centers of provincial England. In those flourishing cities the leading members of the Nonconformist chapels were the local captains of industry, the spearheads of municipal reform, and the magnates of the local Liberty party. Nonconformist families such as the Rathbones and Holts of Liverpool, the Chamberlains and Cadburys of Birmingham, the Peases and Backhouses of Darlington, the Salts and Illingworths of Bradford, the Baineses and Kitsons of Leeds formed an urban governing class which, through intermarriage and business and political associations, had national ramifications. Nonconformity instilled in them a strong sense of public as well as private duty. Jeremiah Colman, the Norwich mustard manufacturer, wrote his future wife shortly before their marriage in 1856: "Talents consecrated to God are what the world and the Church wants . . . . I hope we shan't live an idle selfish existence, for I am sure it won't be a happy one if we do, and we must guard against it. Influence, position and wealth are not given for nothing, and we must try and use them as we should wish at the last we had done." In the course of the century the Nonconformist ministry increasingly turned from unworldly pietism to preach the doctrine that political responsibility was a religious duty. R. W. Dale of Birmingham insisted: "In a country like this, where the public business of the state is the private duty of every citizen, those who decline to use their political power are guilty of treachery both to God and to man."

Dale's activity in municipal and national Liberal politics was in striking contrast to the strictly religious interests of his longtime predecessor at Carrs Lane Chapel, John Angell James. This change was typical of orthodox Nonconformists, and it was accompanied by an increasing strain in their relations with their seemingly natural religious allies, the Evangelicals in the Church of England. During the 1860's there was a growing breach between the Evangelicals and the Dissenters. This was partly because many leading Nonconformists, such as Dale, had come into closer sympathy with the tolerant spirit of the Broad Churchmen while the Low Churchmen held their Evangelical orthodoxy with rigidity and even intolerance. The chief source of difference, however, was political, for, "as a rule, the Evangelicals were staunch upholders of what was called 'The Establishment,' and were almost without exception Conservatives."

The later 1860's and the 1870's brought an intensification of the

Liberalism of Nonconformity. The Reform Act of 1867 and the emergence of a Liberal party led by Gladstone and blessed by Bright created conditions which drew Nonconformists more fully into the arena of national politics. The harvest of individualistic Liberalism had its fruits for political Dissent in the abolition of compulsory church-rates, the disestablishment of the Irish Church, and the removal of religious tests at Oxford and Cambridge. Though it originally precipitated a Nonconformist revolt, the Education Act of 1870 proved favorable to Nonconformist interests. Disestablishment of the Church of England was in the air in the 1870's. The Liberal party increasingly became a vehicle for humanitarian and moral causes in which even formerly nonpolitical Dissenters were interested—peace, temperance, repeal of the Contagious Diseases Acts.

Above all, Gladstone approached politics with a moral passion which had an almost idolatrous appeal to Dissenters of all sects and social strata. As earlier with Irish disestablishment and later with Home Rule, Nonconformists in the late 1870's made up the New Model Army of Gladstone's crusade against Bulgarian atrocities and Disraelian imperialism. The Eastern question formed a turning point in Nonconformist as well as English politics. The Nonconformist conscience became one with the national conscience as interpreted by the High Churchman Gladstone. "It is too commonly believed that 'political Dissent' means nothing more nor less than antagonism to the Establishment," wrote J. G. Rogers, a prominent Congregational minister and Liberal politician.

It really means the subordination of politics to Christian principles. One result of this would, in the judgment of Nonconformists, be the removal of all invidious distinctions resting on the ground of religious opinion, but the principle is of much wider application. It covers the entire area of international relations, and here Mr. Gladstone is recognized by the Nonconformists as one of the very few statesmen who feel that the law of Christ is to govern nations as well as individuals.

By 1880 Nonconformity was substantially absorbed into the Liberal party. Even the ancient conservatism of Wesleyan Methodism—never a part of traditional "political Dissent"—was giving way to active Liberalism. At this high tide of political solidarity and enthusiasm in the chapels, the leading Nonconformist newspaper declared:

> Since the beginning of the century . . . it is certain that Britain has, in the intervals of her blindness, had some inspiring visions of the kingdom of justice one day to be established among men, and it is not to be denied that, taken broadly, the Liberal party has striven to follow the fiery pillar of conscience into this promised land. Like all human combinations it has had its good and evil, its truth and fallacy, its times of glory and disgrace. . . . But, speaking generally, it has striven to be "the party of Christ" . . . the party of moral principle as against that of selfish and corrupt interests, the party of peace as against that of violence, the party of popular improvement and reform as against that of resistance to progress, the party of justice as against that of despotic force or social disorder.
>
> And the backbone of this party has been—to speak historically, without partisan reference [to Nonconformity]—the religious Protestantism and Puritanism of England. For a very good reason, because a party whose object is to rule men's actions by a moral principle in legislation and government derives its force from conscience, and from the omnipotence which is behind it. . . . The strength of the Liberal party is, and always has been, in the force of individual and social conscience. It is a power which, like a mighty river in flood, must eventually carry everything before it, since it is in the nature of right to win at last.

If "the party of conscience" was much like a "secular church," certain of the Nonconformist churches tended to acquire the attributes of "political caucuses." The caucus had, in fact, been born among Birmingham Dissenters. But in fusing with the Liberal party, in acquiring the political habit, Nonconformity became more exposed to the fissures which increasingly cleft that party from the 1880's to the First World War. The bulk of the Nonconformists—and especially the Nonconformist ministry—accepted Gladstone's view of Irish Home Rule as a moral issue, but an influential minority followed Chamberlain and Bright, Dale and Spurgeon, into Liberal Unionism. At the turn of the century, another imperial issue, the Boer War, split Dissent more drastically. In both cases political division entailed some dissension within the churches. Of special significance was the personal tragedy of Dr. Dale, probably the finest representative of Victorian Nonconformity. The bitterness engendered by Home Rule caused him to withdraw not only from the pro-Gladstonian Congregational Union in 1888 but also almost entirely from public work. His disillusionment led him to oppose the formation of the potentially political Free Church Councils in 1892 and to warn against the organized interference of churches in politics.

Of all the issues which divided Nonconformists, it was socialism which had the most fateful influence on Nonconformity as a political and religious force. It is well known that the Nonconformist chapel provided one of the seed-beds of the Labour movement, and that Nonconformity helped to awaken the working classes to political consciousness. The early "Lib-Lab" M.P.'s such as Burt, Broadhurst, Arch, Abraham, and Pickard were usually Dissenters and often lay preachers, and they shared the predilections of Nonconformist Radicalism. Nor were middle-class Nonconformists reluctant to modify extreme individualism to meet the demands of municipal efficiency, notably in Birmingham under Chamberlain's leadership, or the challenges of working-class misery, dramatized by another Dissenter in *The Bitter Cry of Outcast London.* But the spread of socialist ideas and the appearance of an Independent Labour party in the 1890's posed a dilemma which neither Nonconformity nor Liberalism was ultimately able to solve. Middle class Nonconformists were torn between, on the one hand, humanitarianism and traditional alliance with the working classes and, on the other hand, self-interest and traditional individualism. There was an unbridgeable chasm between Dr. Clifford's vision of "fellowship with Socialists" and what Joseph Chamberlain once called "the decorous timidity of prosperous Dissent." The leading London Liberal paper probably reflected the attitude of the typical middle-class Dissenter, as it certainly did of Gladstone, in not distributing its enthusiasm equally between the East End docker and the Bulgarian peasant. Despite attempts by some ministers to preach a gospel of "Social Christianity," it seems just to conclude that Nonconformity, on the whole, was and remained basically individualistic.

These tensions within Nonconformity helped to give the Liberal party its ambivalent attitude toward social and economic questions. In the crucial decade of the 1890's the failure of Liberalism to accommodate itself to working-class aspirations was partly owing to the key position of provincial Nonconformists in the party. In the

North—especially in the West Riding of Yorkshire—the local Liberal leaders, who were usually Nonconformists, were often large employers of labor. As a result, the Liberal party appeared to be committed to the point of view of the employers as opposed to that of the employed. Bradford, long a stronghold of Nonconformist Liberalism, is a classic example of the resulting tensions. The M.P. for West Bradford was Alfred Illingworth, rich worsted spinner, ardent Gladstonian, and old-time Nonconformist Radical of national prominence. In the General Election of 1892 he was opposed by an Independent Labour candidate, Ben Tillett, who attacked him as a capitalist and employer. Though Tillett was himself a Nonconformist and had many Nonconformist supporters, organized Nonconformity rallied to the cause of Illingworth, who won the three-cornered race by a narrow margin. A few months later the outraged Bradford Labourites formed a Labour Church, drawing some members from the Dissenting chapels and from those with Dissenting backgrounds. And before the next General Election Illingworth retired from public life, disgusted with what he regarded as the Liberal party's retreat from individualism on economic issues.

Although Nonconformity was weakened by political divisions over socialism and imperialism, it helped to commit the Liberal party to causes which were becoming increasingly uncongenial and even alien to large sections of the new democracy. Liberalism in the 1890's appeared to many working-class voters as a Crotchet Castle, from which dreary teetotaling Dissenters launched raids on pubs, music halls, and politicians cited in divorce cases. In the Parnell affair, Nonconformists were simply defending the universal moral code of older Victorians, but the growing secularism and hedonism of English society was increasingly isolating puritanical Nonconformity. A conscience which criticized Lord Rosebery's horse racing and which considered "the three deadly enemies of England" to be "drink, impurity, and gambling" was not wholly in touch with what the Christian World hopefully called middle-class Puritanism's "newly-organized allies in the army of labour." It was, indeed, the Liberal government's unpopular bills for local veto on the sale of intoxicating liquors which helped to bring on the disastrous Liberal defeat in the General Election of 1895.

When the Liberals finally returned to office ten years later, they were aided by the wave of Nonconformist agitation against the Balfour government's Education Act of 1902. Free Churchmen of all political camps—Gladstonian Home Rulers and Liberal Unionists, pro-Boers and Liberal Imperialists, old-fashioned Radicals and I.L.P. socialists—united against this measure, which they denounced as endowing Anglican schools and putting a hardship on Nonconformist children in "single-school" areas. Dr. Clifford, the prominent Baptist minister whose political career extended from Chartism to Fabianism, led a passive resistance movement in which many Nonconformists refused to pay school rates, preferring the martyrdom of prison or distraint upon their goods. This rebellion, blessed by the Liberal leadership, was the first and mildest of the revolts against lawful authority which rocked Britain before 1914. While the agitation against the Education Act seemed to show the power of Nonconformity, it made organized Nonconformity more political than ever before and modern Free Churchmen are unanimous in condemning the wisdom of passive resistance, with its "cheapening of conscience by making it a "matter of faction."

In retrospect, this last stand of Nonconformity was an artificial resurgence. The seeming strength of Dissent was illusory; its very prosperity concealed an inner weakness. Despite outward signs of vitality, the number of those who regularly attended Nonconformist services steadily declined during the years before the First World War. The falling off was especially marked among the educated and the young. The saying that "a carriage never goes to a meetinghouse for three generations" expressed an ancient truth of English social history. But the last decades of the nineteenth century and the first of the twentieth saw an acceleration of the familiar process by which the upper stratum of Dissent was absorbed into an Anglican and Conservative upper class—a loss no longer accompanied by compensating accessions from the classes below. The full opening of the older universities to Nonconformists in the 1870's opened the way to professional careers and opportunities hitherto inaccessible and hastened the escape of many young nonconformists from what Matthew Arnold called "the prison of Puritanism."

At the beginning of the twentieth century the Nonconformist haute bourgeoisie was losing the local influence which had distinguished it throughout the Victorian era. Through the growth of limited liability companies and outside management, the expanding family firms were abandoning their patriarchal character, with the personal bond between employer and employed. Municipal government could less often rely on the services of the old Nonconformist governing families, partly because these were being edged out by the new working-class democracy and partly because wealth was taking them into the ranks of the landed gentry or an indifferent rentier class. This was a phenomenon lamented by Beatrice Webb, who observed in 1899:

> Munificent public work has been done at Liverpool by some of the wealthy Unitarian families, but these families are petering out, and the sons are not worthy of their fathers. Whether this is inevitable to all families, or the bad effect of two or three generations of luxury, I do not know. The present generation of rich folk want to enjoy themselves, find nothing to resist, no class or creed interest to fight for, so that they have ceased to consider anything but their pleasures.

Nonconformity had, indeed, become rich and was more than ever limited to the prosperous middle class. The passive resistance movement notwithstanding, "militant witness-bearing" was a thing of the past. Dr. Fairbairn complained in 1897: "It is perhaps harder to be a Nonconformist today than it has ever been in the history of England. The very decay of the disabilities from which our fathers suffered has made it harder to us than it was to them to dissent." More bitter was the assertion of a Nonconformist minister writing anonymously in 1909: "Nonconformity is not, it must be confessed, in the way of making saints. That is a secret which it has somehow lost. Its whole atmosphere is not the atmosphere wherein sainthood grows." He attributed this "loss of distinctly spiritual power" to Nonconformity's exclusive absorption in "political activity for political ends."

This sense of spiritual loss, admitted by the few, was accompanied by a more general feeling of political frustration. Had the Nonconformists delivered their conscience into the keeping of the National Liberal Federation? Had Dr. Dale been a prophet without honor in his warning that "the interference of organized churches with organized political societies has proved after all a false method of effecting the great objects of the Christian gospel"? The fact that after 1906 almost two hundred Free Churchmen were sitting in the House of Commons and that the Liberal front bench was to a marked degree Nonconformist in origin reflected the social complexion of Liberalism rather than the power of Nonconformity. Nor could that formidable phalanx force a new Education Bill, a Licensing Bill, or Welsh disestablishment through the House of Lords. The years after 1906 were years of disappointment and frustration for Free Churchmen. The failure of three Liberal ministers in their attempts to redress educational grievances was especially galling. "Some of us felt at the time that they did not try very hard," a leading Congregational preacher recalled after some thirty years had passed. Though supporting the Liberals against the Lords in the second General Election of 1910, W. R. Nicoll, the editor of the *British Weekly* and a personal friend of Lloyd George, privately admitted that "politicians on either side have done nothing for us."

On the eve of the war, Nonconformity, like official Liberalism, was politically exhausted and divided and hesitant as to the future. The issues in which Nonconformists were peculiarly interested, such as education and Welsh disestablishment, were only surface irritants outside of Wales. The old demand for disestablishment of the Church of England had all but disappeared. Temperance and other moral reforms associated with the Nonconformist conscience were even less popular and less representative of English opinion than they had been twenty years earlier. The so-called "middle-class morality" was being challenged not only by Shavian wit but by social practice. Religion no longer held the primary place in the lives of most Englishmen. For religious people, the vital issue was not church vs. chapel, but Christianity vs. unbelief. Dissent no longer carried with it a significant burden of legal or social disability. This emancipation of Nonconformists was a triumph of the Liberalism whose root was "respect for the dignity and worth of the individual." But when the iron went out of the soul of Nonconformity—when Dissent ceased to dissent—the robust vitality of traditional Liberalism was weakened.

The Liberal government, which had come into office on the old issues of free trade and church vs. chapel, attempted to meet the problems of the new century with collectivistic measures at home and alliances abroad. Though they showed a constructive vigor, these departures from the Gladstonian faith left many Liberals uncomfortable survivors from the Victorian past. Sir Edward Grey's foreign policy, in particular, evoked exasperated protests from the Liberal press and provincial Liberalism. More significant, from 1910 on the government had to lead a country paralyzed by factional disputes unprecedented since the 1830's. The revolt of the Conservatives over the Lloyd George budget and the Parliament Bill, the rise of syndicalism and the spread of strikes, the fury of the militant suffragettes, the defiance of Ulster and the threat of civil war in Ireland over the Home Rule Bill—all were rending the fabric of British society on the eve of the First World War. These struggles posed problems and involved methods with which Liberalism, based on government by discussion, was neither accustomed to deal nor able to cope. The coming of the war freed the Asquith government from these ordeals, but it added a new burden under which Liberalism collapsed. The war completed the undermining of the secure world in which Liberalism had performed its work. As has been seen, however, even before 1914 the decline of Nonconformity had as an inevitable consequence the decline of Liberalism. The ebbing of the Nonconformist conscience entailed the gradual loss of the Liberal party's practical political strength and, more important, the loss of the religious ethos and moral passion which had distinguished English Liberalism in its creative golden age.

Joseph Chamberlain
MUNICIPAL SOCIALISM

The most influential and controversial Nonconformist politician of the nineteenth century was Joseph Chamberlain (1836–1914). As an industrialist, mayor, and political organizer, he transformed Birmingham into a model of municipal socialism. Elected to Parliament in 1876, he rose rapidly in influence and provided liberalism with a social radicalism which produced an

(I) From Charles E. Boyd (ed.), *Mr. Chamberlain's Speeches,* 2 volumes (London: Constable and Company, Ltd., 1914), Vol. I, pp. 161–166, Reprinted by permission of Constable and Company, Ltd. (II) *Ibid.,* Vol. I, pp. 168–170. Reprinted by permission of Constable and Company, Ltd. (III) From Joseph Chamberlain, *The Radical Platform* (Edinburgh: n.p., 1885), pp. 22–23.

*"unauthorized programme" in 1885 that by no means endeared him to ortho-
dox liberals. Impatient with his colleagues who seemed to be looking back-
ward to a golden age, he turned to state action as the remedy for the social
ills of the laissez-faire state. Inevitably, his personality and program pro-
voked controversy. Called a socialist, a communist, a liberal radical, and a
political opportunist, Chamberlain seldom conciliated his opponents; he
seemed to delight in enraging them. His attacks on the "cant of selfish
wealth" and his defense of the Radical Program are the focal points in the
three speeches that follow.*

(I)

Speech at the Eighty Club, April 28, 1885

Now, there are two ways in which politics may be regarded. By
many men the pursuit of politics is avowedly treated as a great game
of personal ambition—not altogether ignoble, not entirely selfish,
but pursued chiefly as an occupation for capable minds, and as varying with its excitement the ordinary monotony of life. But, then, to a
large and ever-increasing number of persons politics is the science
of social happiness, as its half-sister, political economy, is the science of social wealth; and to these men the pursuit of politics viewed
in this sense is a duty which is cast upon all who desire to raise the
general condition of those among whom they live—and political influence is the chief, if it be not the only instrument by which any
large amelioration of unfavourable circumstances, and any extensive
improvement in the condition of the masses of the population, can
possibly be secured.

Whichever view we take, one thing is clear, that new considerations have come into the view of politicians, and in consequence of
recent reforms they will have to enlarge the sources of their inspiration and to seek guidance and light from new quarters. The people
at large have become, or will become the true source and deposi-
tory of power. . . . Whether we like it or not, the wishes and the
wants—ay, and the rights—of the whole people will have to be
considered. . . .

To hear some people talk, one would suppose that this is really
the best of all possible worlds, and that the only thing for a Liberal
to do is to cultivate his own garden for himself. I do not think that

the circumstances justify the optimism of Candide. Just let me take one or two facts in our boasted civilisation. It is perfectly true that political economy has every reason to be satisfied with itself. The aggregate wealth of the country has increased in a degree and proportion for which the most sanguine of our predecessors was not in the slightest degree prepared. The accumulation of capital has been enormous. The progress of science and invention has multiplied our comforts and has increased our luxuries. Trade has advanced in giant strides out of all proportion to our population. That is one side of the picture. But continuously and concurrently with that there are always one million, or very nearly a million, of persons in receipt of parish relief. There are more than one million others on the verge of pauperism, who, in times of depression like these, and at any moment of bad trade, are subject to the most desperate privations. The whole class of the agricultural labourers of this country is never able to do more than make both ends meet, and they have to look forward in the time of illness or on the approach of old age to the workhouse as the one inevitable refuge against starvation. Tens of thousands of households do not know the luxury of milk. Children are stunted in their growth and dulled in their intellects for want of proper nourishment and proper food, and the houses of the poor are so scanty and insufficient that grievous immorality prevails, which seldom comes to the surface, but which is known to all those who move among the poor. The ordinary conditions of life among a large proportion of the population are such that common decency is absolutely impossible; and all this goes on in sight of the mansions of the rich, where undoubtedly there are people who would gladly remedy it if they could. . . .

These things are proved to be a disgrace to our legislation; and yet we have found it possible, perhaps even convenient, to ignore them. I say, when I think of these things, it is not enough to sneer at the enthusiasm of men who find their hearts moved with indignation at evils which, perhaps, they are not wise enough to cure. It is not enough to treat these as the inevitable incidents of the struggle for existence—the natural concomitants of our complex civilisation. It is not enough to discourage every well-meant effort for reform, and to stand before the people and propose no substitute as a remedy.

. . . I ask you not to be afraid of words. Because the doctrine of natural rights was abused in the time of the French Revolution, do not ignore the fundamental right which every man holds in common for a chance of decent existence, but try rather to give it the sanction of law and authority, for it has the eternal foundations of justice and equity. Because State Socialism may cover very injurious and very unwise theories, that is not reason at all why we should refuse to recognise the fact that Government is only the organisation of the whole people for the benefit of all its members, and that the community may—ay, and ought to—provide for all its members benefits which it is impossible for individuals to provide by their solitary and separate efforts. I venture to say that it is only the community acting as a whole that can possibly deal with evils so deep-seated as those to which I have referred. When Government represented only the authority of the Crown or the views of a particular class, I can understand that it was the first duty of men who valued their freedom to restrict its authority and to limit its expenditure. But all that is changed. Now Government is the organised expression of the wishes and the wants of the people, and under these circumstances let us cease to regard it with suspicion.

. . . The general principles, then, to which, in conclusion, I invite your attention are these:—In the first place I urge upon you a full recognition of the magnitude of the evils with which we have to deal; in the second place, I insist on the right of those who suffer to redress; and in the third place, I assert the duty of society as a whole to secure the comfort and welfare of all its individual members. As a consequence of this, in the next place, I desire to submit to you that it belongs to the authority and to the duty of the State— that is to say, of the whole people acting through their chosen representatives—to utilise for this purpose all local experience and all local organisation, to protect the weak, and to provide for the poor, to redress the inequalities of our social system, to alleviate the harsh conditions of the struggle for existence, and to raise the average enjoyment of the majority of the population.

*   *   *

(II)

Speech at Hull, August 5, 1885

I believe that the great evil with which we have to deal is the excessive inequality in the distribution of riches. Ignorance, intemperance, immorality, and disease—these things are all interdependent and closely connected; and although they are often the cause of poverty, they are still more frequently the consequence of destitution, and if we can do anything to raise the condition of the poor in this country, to elevate the masses of the people, and give them the means of enjoyment and recreation, to afford to them opportunities of improvement, we should do more for the prosperity, ay, for the morality of this country than anything we can do by laws, however stringent, for the prevention of excess, or the prevention of crime. I want you to make this the first object in the Liberal programme for the reformed Parliament. . . .

I am not a Communist, although some people will have it that I am. Considering the difference in the character and the capacity of men, I do not believe that there can ever be an absolute equality of conditions, and I think that nothing would be more undesirable than that we should remove the stimulus to industry and thrift and exertion which is afforded by the security given to every man in the enjoyment of the fruits of his own individual exertions. I am opposed to confiscation in every shape or form, because I believe that it would destroy that security, and lessen that stimulus. But, on the other hand, I am in favour of accompanying the protection which is afforded to property with a large and stringent interpretation of the obligations of property. . . .

I look for great results from the development of local government amongst us. The experience of the great towns is very encouraging in this respect. By their wise and liberal use of the powers entrusted to them, they have, in the majority of cases, protected the health of the community; they have provided means of recreation and enjoyment and instruction, and they have done a great deal to equalise social advantages, and to secure for all the members of the community the enjoyments which, without their aid and assistance, would have been monopolised by the rich alone. You have, in connection with the great municipal corporations, hospitals, schools, museums, free libraries, art galleries, baths, parks. All these things which a generation ago could only have been obtained by the well-to-do, are now, in many large towns, placed at the service of every citizen by the action of the municipalities. I desire that the opportunity should be afforded to the whole country, and I think that, having regard to what has been done in the past, we may show great confidence in the work of popular representative bodies, and be contented to extend their functions and increase their powers and authority.

(III)

Speech at the Public Hall, Warrington, September 8, 1885

There is not a single Liberal candidate who has not accepted some one or more points of the Radical programme. It is therefore perfectly futile and ridiculous for any political Rip Van Winkle to come down from the mountain on which he has been slumbering, and to tell us that these things are to be excluded from the Liberal programme. The world has moved on whilst these dreamers have been sleeping, and it would be absurd to ignore the growth of public opinion, and the change in the situation which the Reform Acts have produced.

I do not wish you to think that I desire to rest my case upon political necessity alone. If we cannot convince our allies of the justice and reasonableness of our views, then, with whatever reluctance, we must part company; we will fight alone; we will appeal unto Caesar; we will go to the people from whom we come and whose cause we plead; and, although the verdict may be delayed, I, for my part, have not one shadow of doubt as to the ultimate decision. We have been looking to the extension of the franchise in order to bring into prominence questions which have been too long neglected. The great problem of our civilisation is still unresolved. We have to account for and to grapple with the mass of misery and destitution in our midst, co-existent as it is with the evidence of abundant wealth and teeming prosperity. It is a problem which some men would put aside by reference to the eternal laws of supply and demand, to the necessity of freedom of contract, and to the sanctity of every private right of property. But, gentlemen, these phrases are the convenient cant of selfish wealth. . . . These are no answers to our questions. I quite understand the reason for timidity in dealing with this question so long as Government was merely the expression of the will of a prejudiced and limited few. . . . But now that we have a Government of the people by the people, we will go on and we will make it for every man his natural right—his right to existence, and to a fair enjoyment of it. I shall be told tomorrow that this is Socialism. . . . Of course, it is Socialism. The Poor-Law is Socialism. The Education Act is Socialism. The greater part of municipal work is Socialism, and every kindly act of legislation by which the community has sought to discharge its responsibilities and its obligations to the poor is Socialism, but is none the worse for that. Our object is the elevation of the poor, of the masses of the people—a levelling up, by which we shall do something to remove the excessive inequality in social life which is now one of the greatest dangers. . . . I do not pretend that for every grievance a remedy will be found. We must try experiments as we are bound to do . . . and if we fail, let us try again and again and again until we succeed.

George Sabine
SPENCER'S SCIENTIFIC LAWS OF LIBERALISM

Few English philosophers have ever planned their schema on so vast a scale as did Herbert Spencer (1820–1903). By 1857 Spencer, after an earlier career as a railway engineer and a journalist, had projected a system of philosophy which, he asserted, would prove the dangerous errors of "the so-called Liberalism of the present." Symbolizing his antipathy toward central authority was the title of one of his books, The Man Versus the State *(1884).*

From Chapter XXXII, from *A History of Political Theory*, 3rd ed., by George H. Sabine, pp. 721–725. Copyright 1937, 1950, © 1961 by Holt, Rinehart and Winston, Inc. Copyright © 1965 by George B. Sabine, Janet S. Kelbley, and Mary J. Sabine. Reprinted by permission of Holt, Rinehart and Winston, Inc., and George G. Harrap & Co., Ltd.

His other works include Social Statics *(1850) and* Principles of Biology *(1864–1867). Spencer's conception of organic evolution captured the popular imagination by applying Darwin's theory of natural selection to social institutions. The legitimacy of his "scientific" formula and his contribution to liberal theory are highlighted in the following selection from the political philosopher, George Sabine, who, in 1947, concluded forty-one years of distinguished teaching, largely at Cornell University.*

For the purpose of gauging the state of liberal theory in the third quarter of the nineteenth century, it is both interesting and instructive to compare the philosophy of Mill with that of Herbert Spencer. The two men were generally recognized as the most important exponents of the philosophy of political liberalism and of the native British philosophical tradition. Both had their intellectual origins in Philosophical Radicalism. In the case of Spencer this was not quite as evident as in the case of Mill because he put at the center of his philosophy the new conception of organic evolution. Yet all of Spencer's important ethical and political ideas were derived from utilitarianism and had no close logical dependence on either biology or evolution. The *Social Statics* was published nine years before Darwin's *Origin of Species,* and to a considerable degree Spencer's later evolutionary ethics consisted in constructing speculative psychological ties between pleasure and biological survival. . . .

Spencer carried on into the latter part of the nineteenth century the rationalist tradition of the classical economists and utilized evolution to reconstruct the system of a natural society with natural boundaries between economics and politics. Yet a substantial part of what both Spencer and Mill did for social philosophy was to reach out for new intellectual connections and to break down the insularity of the older liberalism. In the case of Spencer this consisted in bringing it into relation with biology and sociology and with biological and social evolution.

Spencer's Synthetic Philosophy was an astonishing system of nineteenth-century rationalism (covering the whole range of knowledge from physics to ethics) worked out through thirty-five years and ten volumes, and constructed with no important change of plan between the prospectus and the concluding volume. Nothing analogous to it can easily be found short of the great systems of natural law that flourished in the seventeenth century, and indeed the intellectual affinities between these and Spencer's philosophy were close. For Spencer the modernized version of "nature" was evolution. . . . Assuming "the instability of the homogeneous" Spencer undertook the amazing task of "deducing" organic evolution from the conservation of energy. And from this beginning the system proceeded successively to the principles of biology, of psychology, of sociology, and of ethics. Allowing for temporary eddies of "dissolution," nature advances upon a straight line from energy to life, from life to mind, from mind to society, from society to civilization and to more highly differentiated and integrated civilizations.

It need hardly be said that this kind of logical *tour de force* was not notable for its scientific rigor or for the cogency of its deductions. In a large measure it was in its own day an astonishingly successful popularization, and it has suffered the fate of obsolete popularizations. In a sense it was typical of its period, even though few thinkers attempted a philosophical synthesis so broad. . . . It expressed again the hope that the growth of society would provide clear criteria of lower and higher stages of development by which to distinguish the obsolete from the suitable, the fit from the unfit, and therefore the good from the bad. With Spencer this hope was given the appearance of having behind it the established fact of organic evolution, since moral improvement was made to seem merely an extension of the biological concept of adaptation, and social well-being appeared to be equated with the survival of the fittest.

The only way in which Spencer could pass from biological adaptation to moral progress was by supposing that socially valuable behavior, once established by moral prescription as habits, is translated into anatomical changes that are transmitted by inheritance. This belief, of which Spencer was a lifelong exponent, was not only biologically baseless but was the source of endless confusion about the nature of culture and of social change. Yet when all this has been said about the deficiencies of Spencer's philosophy, it must still in fairness be added that it contributed to important changes in the social studies, quite without reference to the validity of particular conclusions. It brought psychology into relation with biology, and this was a first step toward breaking down the dogmatism of the old associational psychology. It also brought politics and ethics into the context of sociological and anthropological investigation and therefore into the context of cultural history. . . . Spencer like Mill, though in a different way, broke down the intellectual isolation of the older utilitarian philosophy and of social studies in general, making them a part of the broad sweep of modern science.

Spencer's political philosophy on the other hand was merely reactionary. He remained a philosophical radical after philosophical radicalism had been obsolete for a generation. The theory of evolution provided him with the concept of a "natural" society, and this turned out to be only a new version of the old system of natural liberty. The deduction presented some difficulties, since it might seem that evolution would make the state, like society, more complex and more highly integrated, while Spencer had to prove that a society which grew steadily more complex would support a state that simplified itself practically out of existence. He solved the paradox by supposing that most functions exercised by government originated in a military society and that war would become obsolete in an industrialized society. Hence he inferred that, with increased industrialization, more and more would be left to private enterprise. Indeed Spencer's theory of the state was very largely a list of functions that the state should at once abandon, since they had been assumed in the first place by some of the innumerable "sins of legislators," or of functions that will be made unnecessary by the progress of evolution. . . .

Most legislation is bad, because it mars the perfection which nature tends to produce by the survival of the fittest, and virtually all legislation will be rendered obsolete as evolution approaches a perfect adaptation of the individual to society. Hence Spencer opposed consistently all regulation of industry, including sanitary regulations or the requirement of safety devices, all forms of public charity, and public support for education. Indeed, in the *Social Statics* he proposed that the state should turn over the mint and the post office to private enterprise.

The philosophies of Mill and Spencer taken together left the theory of liberalism in a state of unintelligible confusion. Mill restated its philosophy in such a way as to suggest that he departed in no important way from the principles of his father and of Bentham, but he so qualified the conclusions that they gave little or no support to what had always been deemed to be the characteristic line of liberal policy, namely, the limitation of control by governments, the encouragement of private enterprise, and the widest possible extension of freedom of contract. Spencer on the contrary had given to liberalism a new philosophy that purported to depend upon a scientific discovery unknown to any generation before his own, but the new philosophy turned out to teach more rigidly than ever before a policy that practical liberals, who were not overly concerned about logical consistency, had already discovered to need substantial modifications. In either case the French proverb seemed to apply: *Plus ça change, plus c'est la même chose.* Liberalism seemed to be a set of formulas that had ceased to mean what they had always been thought to mean and a set of policies that corresponded to no formulas at all. Yet two facts were evident to any clear-thinking person of liberal sympathies. One was that the enfranchisement and organization of labor were giving political power to a class that had no intention of accepting without a struggle anyone's demonstration that its standard of living was fixed permanently at the level of existence and reproduction, without the amenities that industrialism was producing in ever larger volume. The other was that public opinion, whether on ethical or religious or humanitarian grounds, was prepared to countenance and support this claim. With the results of unregulated industrialism before it, a new generation of liberals was not prepared to acquiesce in the belief that government has only a negative role to play in making men free. . . . What was evidently needed was a re-examination of the philosophy which supported the ideals of a liberal society and the function in it of a liberal government.

Crane Brinton
MORAL IDEALISM AND T. H. GREEN

Thomas Hill Green (1836–1882), Fellow of Balliol College, Oxford, radically altered the liberal assumptions relating to the individual and the state. He argued that positive state action was not a threat but a necessity to the moral self-realization of the individual, and his influence worked a fundamental revolution in English liberalism. Drawing his inspiration from Plato and Hegel, the Oxford professor enlisted hundreds of young followers for his version of liberalism. They, in turn, popularized and politicized his philosophical schema. One of his admirers was the late Crane Brinton, a Rhodes scholar, and popular professor of history at Harvard University whose works include Ideas and Men *and* The Shaping of the Modern Mind. *Brinton's sympathies for Green and his reformulation of liberalism are evident in the following selection.*

No one, not even the Mill who wrote so sympathetically of Socialism in his later years, marks better than Thomas Hill Green the change which came over English Liberalism in the latter half of the nineteenth century. Green himself wrote in 1881:

> There is a noticeable difference between the present position of political reformers and that in which they stood a generation ago. Then they fought the fight of reform in the name of individual freedom against class privilege. Their opponents could not with any plausibility invoke the same name against them. Now, in appearance—though as I shall try to show, not in reality—the case is changed. The nature of the genuine political reformer is perhaps always the same. The passion for improving mankind, in its ultimate object, does not vary. . . . [It is] the same old cause of social good against class interests, for which, under altered names, liberals are fighting now as they fought fifty years ago.

The methods are different, but the goal is the same. Legal regulation of wages aims at freedom as much as did the abolition of the Corn Laws.

Green held that his idealist metaphysics provided the necessary basis for the transition from *laissez-faire* to State regulation, that through a proper philosophy the new freedom would be seen to be

From Crane Brinton, *English Political Thought in the Nineteenth Century*, 2nd ed. (London: Ernest Benn, Ltd., 1949), pp. 212, 214–223, 225–226. Excerpted by permission of the publishers, Ernest Benn, Ltd., and Harvard University Press.

but the inevitable development of the old. Whether we agree with him or not will depend on our own estimate of the importance of metaphysics.

*   *   *

At the very start of his political philosophy, Green comes to grips with the problem of freedom. He is too good an Englishman to dismiss with contempt the common-sense notion that, metaphysics put aside, a man is free when he does at any given moment what at that moment he wants to do. So, too, political freedom may be given the common-sense definition of the exemption of the individual in doing what he wants to do from the interference of any other individual or individuals. But Green is perfectly aware of the barrenness of such common-sense definitions. In what sense is the man who drinks himself to death a free man? Must we not say that "it is one thing when the object in which self-satisfaction is sought is such as to prevent that self-satisfaction being found, because interfering with the realization of the seeker's possibilities or his progress towards perfection; it is another thing when it contributes to this end"? In the former case, he is free in the common-sense definition—he does what he wants to do. But in another sense he is not free, for his will to arrive at self-satisfaction is not adjusted to the law which determines where this self-satisfaction is to be found. The drunkard is a bondsman who is carrying out the will of another, not his own. . . . "Hence, as in Plato, the terms 'freedom' and 'bondage' may be used to express a relation between the man on the one side, as distinguishing himself from all impulses that do not tend to his true good, and those impulses on the other. He is a 'slave' when they are masters of him, 'free' when master of them."

The way is thus open for us, if we like, to say with Hegel that true freedom, as the condition in which the will is determined by an object adequate to itself, is realized in the State. Such a State may be regarded as "objective freedom," as incorporating the attainable perfection of a higher reason than is found in the individual. Submission to law as defined by the State is thus really liberty, and we can aptly employ Rousseau's paradoxical phrase about forcing a man to be free. With this position Green finds himself to a certain extent sympathetic. He accepts to the full the Aristotelian position that the State is "natural" and therefore moral, that the accumulated efforts of generations of men striving to translate their aspirations into reality, their *values* into *facts,* have built up a nexus of social relations which definitely embodies the good life, and to which, therefore, the good man will on the whole conform. But he is shocked by the full collectivist implications of the Hegelian position, by its sacrifice of the individual to the State, by its easy adaptability to such unpleasant formulas as "whatever is, is right" and "might makes right." He insists that "we cannot significantly speak of freedom except with reference to individual persons; that only in them can freedom be realized; that therefore the realization of freedom in the State can only mean the attainment of freedom by individuals through influence which the State . . . supplies." Surely in any given State such a realization of freedom has been most imperfect. "To an Athenian slave, who might be used to gratify a master's lust, it would have been a mockery to speak of the state as a realization of freedom; and perhaps it would not be much less so to speak of it as such to an untaught and underfed denizen of a London yard with gin-shops on the right hand and on the left." Hegelian idealism too easily identifies aspiration with fact. . . .

We may, then—nay, we must, if we are to avoid the Hegelian deification of the State—distinguish logically between moral freedom and political freedom. The individual is politically free when, by an act of imaginative reason, he accepts the whole nexus of social relations as a necessary guide, when he realizes that his own good must also be the common good. Incompletely, if you like, from the point of view of the ideal, but none the less genuinely for mortal beings, the State is founded upon will. Therefore what we know as self-government, or democracy, is for a people capable of it the highest form of government, a government towards which all peoples must strive. Fear, if only fear of the policeman, is even to-day a necessary concomitant of government; but the less fear enters into civil obedience, the better the government.

Accepting the State as a moral force, admitting the existence of the general will, we have now to consider two important related problems which cover the essentials of politics: what are the limits of the power of the group—that is, the power of the group acting socially through convention, as well as acting politically through law

—over the individual; and how far can such power be used to promote pure morality?

The first problem may be put in this way: when may the individual be said to have the right to resist the group? Now "a right against society, in distinction from a right to be treated as member of society, is a contradiction in terms." The trouble with the eighteenth century was that in the name of a misunderstood "Nature," it set the individual crudely in opposition to the State. There are indeed individual rights, and we may call them "innate" or "natural," but only in the Aristotelian sense that the State itself is natural. These rights "arise out of, and are necessary for the fulfilment of, a moral capacity without which a man would not be a man." Stripped of their dogmatic assertiveness and their false philosophical origins, these rights are substantially what the last century thought them to be. In a parliamentary State like England, these rights are pretty substantially equivalent to the fabric of existing law. Therefore a modern Englishman has not a right to resist the law. In the first place, any existing social system incorporates the efforts of so many generations of men, is so thoroughly in accordance with the national character, that the presumption must be in its favour against even a very wise individual. Moreover, resistance to a single law is apt to end in resistance to the whole fabric of the law, in an attempt at complete revolution. If an Englishman is convinced that a law is a bad one, his duty is to agitate against it, to attempt by legal propaganda to secure its repeal. If he thinks a custom a bad one, he may refuse to conform to it, though he must never lose sight of the fact that his brethren may find it a necessary limitation. But there are four cases, none of which apply to modern England, where the individual has a right to resist. First, where the legality of a given command is doubtful. In the United States, for instance, the States rights question is so involved that there is nothing to amount to a real right in either the State or the federal side, and the good citizen may obey whichever authority his conscience directs him to obey. Second, where there is no means of agitating for the repeal or alteration of a law. Here resistance is not only a right, but a duty. Third, where the whole system of government is so perverted by private, selfish interests hostile to the public, that temporary anarchy brought on by revolution is preferable to the maintenance of the existing order. Fourth, where the authority commanding is so easily separated from the whole system of rights and order that the latter will not be affected by resistance to a particular law. But the good man, who is also a humble man, will hesitate long before he resists the State. Revolutionists are forced to "go it blind," and incur consequences beyond the power of our intelligence to predict.

Our second problem is this: how far can the State, acting through concrete laws enforced by its police power, promote morality? Now the essential point about Liberalism is that it aims at increasing moral freedom for the individual. The root idea even of *laissez-faire* Liberalism is sound: the individual must help himself. Paternalism, well-meant autocracy, is bad because it keeps him like a child in leading-strings, because it atrophies his moral strength. But the Manchester school [of Political Economy, which endorsed complete free trade and non-interference by the government in the economy], barred by their atomistic view of the individual, have missed an important distinction. The State ought indeed to remove many of the historic restraints on free dealing between man and man, for such restraints, though rising partly perhaps from some confused idea of maintaining morality, have arisen much more from the power of class-interests. But its purpose must be the *removing of obstacles to morality*; and such a removing may often mean positive legislative enactments enjoining specific performances—that is, legislation quite contrary to the programme of *laissez-faire.* For instance: an ignorant man cannot be morally autonomous, cannot to-day be a good citizen. But it is clear that not all parents will voluntarily make the sacrifices necessary to educate their children. Therefore a compulsory system of education, showing due respect for the preferences, ecclesiastical and otherwise, of the parents, must be set up by the State. Such a compulsion will not deaden spontaneity, for it is only felt as compulsion by those who have, in this respect, no spontaneity to interfere with. Again, there is the principle of freedom of contract. "The freedom to do as they like on the part of one set of men may involve the ultimate disqualification of many others, or of a succeeding generation, for the exercise of rights. This applies most obviously to such kinds of contract or traffic as affect the health and housing of the people, the growth of population relatively to the means of subsistence, and the accumulation or distribution of landed property." The results of a contract freely entered into by weak or ignorant men may be such as to place insuperable obstacles in the way of their attaining moral freedom. Such for instance is the "contract" between the Irish landlord and his tenant. "To uphold the sanctity of contracts is doubtless a prime business of government, but it is no less its business to provide against contracts being made, which from the helplessness of one of the parties to them, instead of being a security for freedom, become an instrument of disguised oppression." . . .

The way is thus open to consider some of the practical problems of our present society. Recognizing that the State has a positive, and not merely a negative, function, that the current attitude which condemns all legislation beyond the bare repression of crimes of violence is short-sighted and wrong, we can ask ourselves what sort of legislation the good citizen should promote.

In the first place, at least in England, he will work for universal suffrage. Only through active participation in the affairs of State does a man become a citizen, and capable of improving himself. Parliament must cease to be a "rich man's club," though it be necessary to provide for payment of members. It is true that a completely democratic Parliament may be a tyrannical Parliament. From the dangers of a centralized democracy on the French pattern, England, however, has been hitherto singularly free. The diversity of English group life must be preserved. . . .

Education must be a primary concern of the English Liberal. Like Matthew Arnold, Green felt that the heart of the problem lay in the education of the newly enriched industrial classes. Nettleship writes that "his strongest sympathies were with the education of the middle classes, whom the universities were just beginning to touch. An undercurrent of indignant pity for the intellectual condition of these classes pervades his writings. . . . The monopoly of the gentry at Oxford and Cambridge must be destroyed. Open scholarships must be increased, and the snobbishness of the public school element broken down." . . .

In economic life, Liberalism must go a long way towards what an older generation would have called Socialism or Communism. We have had Factory Acts and sanitary legislation even during the reign of the Manchester school. If we take as our guiding rule that the

State should interfere not to coddle the workman, not to encourage his vices by protecting them, as did the old Poor Law, but to remove obstacles to self-help, our path is fairly clear. "Every injury to the health of the individual is, so far as it goes, a public injury. It is an impediment to the general freedom; so much deduction from our power, as members of society, to make the best of ourselves. Society is, therefore, plainly within its right when it limits freedom of contract for the sale of labour, so far as is done by our laws for the sanitary regulation of factories, workshops, and mines." Therefore, as Liberals, we shall encourage labour unions, co-operative societies, the various forms of social insurance (exacting a share of the premiums from the workman himself), regulation of the liquor trade, and similar measures. We shall, as privileged by our wealth and education, encourage wise private charities, even more, take part ourselves in the work of social service.

*   *   *

Green's services to English Liberalism were very great. His actual programme, as we have outlined it, can be seen to be not very different, save in respect to the temperance question, from that which was gradually forcing itself on all English parties. But the differences between the Tory temperament and the Liberal temperament are very real ones. The Tory, however much he may sympathize with democracy, is at bottom a patriarch. He will not give up the richness of social gradation he sees in the past. The Liberal, on the other hand, however much he may inveigh against Socialism, is at bottom an egalitarian. He is always a little indifferent, or hostile, to the past. Compare Disraeli's sense of the immanence of the seventeenth century in the nineteenth with Green's statement that in the Civil War "neither our conservatism nor our liberalism, neither our oligarchic nor our 'levelling' zeal, can find much to claim as its own in a struggle which was for a hierarchy under royal licence on the one side, and for a freedom founded in grace on the other."

Now a weakness of mid-nineteenth-century Liberalism, in so far as it stemmed from Benthamism, was that it lacked a metaphysical superstructure flexible enough to permit it to adapt itself to changing conditions. Not even Mill . . . could supply his followers with a faith, with an imaginative interpretation of the facts of common life. Green did just that. Idealism may seem to the sceptic so willing to adapt itself to the varying exigencies of daily life that he is inclined to dismiss it as a cheat, a mere disguise. But that is a shallow view. Green's idealism, applied to the drinker facing a public house closed by the Government, may not get much beyond forcing a man to be free. But empiricism here can but analyse the difficulty; it cannot solve it. Men do solve it, for purposes of getting along, by accommodating their desires to their imagination. By an act of faith, in most hardly distinguishable from habit, they submit to a common weal with which they identify themselves. Faith lives upon sacrifice and limitation. The trouble with Benthamism was that it did not provide for sacrifice and limitation. It roundly asserted the identity of the interests of the individual and the interests of the group. Green, more than any other Englishman, succeeded in reconciling the Benthamite temper with the necessities of a faith. His influence at Oxford was very great indeed. He not only, through such men as Bosanquet, perpetuated his influence among leaders of thought. He worked upon the imagination of hundreds of young men who were to do the work of English politics, and enlisted them for the new Liberalism. In the opinion of a doctrinaire like Spencer, indeed, he gave up all that was good in Liberalism. But if we hold the test of individual liberty to be even more a matter of faith than a matter of fact, if we hold that our senses can only so far be free as our imagination is disciplined, if we hold that even a pragmatic balance between liberty and authority must pay its tribute to mysticism, we must regard Green as one of the saviours of Liberalism.

III THE NEW LIBERALISM

David G. Ritchie
PHILOSOPHY OF STATE INTERFERENCE

*The old liberal antithesis between the individual and the state is altogether
missing in David G. Ritchie's* Principles of State Interference *(1891). At the
time Ritchie (1853–1903) was a fellow of Jesus College, Oxford. Three years
later he became professor of logic and metaphysics at St. Andrews University. Ritchie's "higher stage" of liberalism is based on the assumption that
the individual and the state can grow in freedom together without one growing greater at the expense of the other.*

Underlying all these traditions and prejudices [in favor of the individual and suspicious of the state] there is a particular metaphysical
theory—a metaphysical theory which takes hold of those persons
especially who are fondest of abjuring all metaphysics; and the
disease is in their case the more dangerous since they do not know
when they have it. The chief symptom of this metaphysical complaint
is the belief in the abstract individual. The individual is thought of,
at least spoken of, as if he had a meaning and significance apart
from his surroundings and apart from his relations to the community
of which he is a member. It may be quite true that the significance
of the individual is not exhausted by his relations to any given set of
surroundings; but apart from all of these he is a mere abstraction—
a logical ghost, a metaphysical spectre, which haunts the habitations
of those who have derided metaphysics. The individual, apart from
all relations to a community, is a negation. You can say nothing
about him, or rather it, except that it is not any other individual.
Now, along with this negative and abstract view of the individual
there goes, as counterpart, the way of looking at the State as an
opposing element to the individual. The individual and the State are
put over against one another. Their relation is regarded as one
merely of antithesis. Of course, this is a point of view which we can
take, and quite rightly for certain purposes; but it is only one point
of view. It expresses only a partial truth; and a partial truth, if accepted as the whole truth, is always a falsehood. Such a conception

From David G. Ritchie, *The Principles of State Interference* (London: Swan Sonnen-
schein & Co., Ltd., 1891), pp. 11–12, 62–64.

is, in any case, quite inadequate as a basis for any profitable discussion of the duties of Government.

It is this theory of the individual which underlies Mill's famous book, *On Liberty*. Mill, and all those who take up his attitude toward the State, seem to assume that all power gained by the State is so much taken from the individual; and, conversely, that all power gained by the individual is gained at the expense of the State. Now this is to treat the two elements, power of the State and power (or liberty) of the individual, as if they formed the debit and credit sides of an account book; it is to make them like two heaps of a fixed number of stones, to neither of which can you add without taking from the other. It is to apply a mere quantitative conception in politics, as if that were an adequate "category" in such matters.

*   *   *

Life Mr. Spencer defines as adaptation of the individual to his environment; but, unless the individual manages likewise to adapt his environment to himself, the definition would be more applicable to death.

It must not be supposed that we wish to blind ourselves to the many real difficulties and objections which there are in the way of remedying and preventing evils by direct State action. If assured that the end is good, we must see that the means are sufficient and necessary, and we must be prepared to count the cost. But, admitting the real difficulties, we must not allow imaginary difficulties to block the way. In the first place, . . . State action does not necessarily imply the direct action of the central government. Many things may be undertaken by local bodies which it would be unwise to put under the control of officials at a distance. "Municipalisation" is, in many cases, a much better "cry" than "Nationalisation." Experiments may also be more safely tried in small than in large areas, and local bodies may profit by each other's experience. Diffusion of power may well be combined with concentration of information. "Power," says J. S. Mill, "may be localised, but knowledge to be most useful must be centralised." Secondly, there are many matters which can more easily be taken in hand than others by the State as at present constituted. Thus the means of communication and locomotion can in every civilised country be easily nationalised or municipalised, where this has not been done already. With regard to productive industries, there may appear greater difficulty. But the process now going by which the individual capitalist more and more gives place to enormous jointstock enterprises, worked by salaried managers, this tendency of capital to become "impersonal," is making the transition to management by government (central or local) very much more simple, and very much more necessary, than in the days of small industries, before the "industrial revolution" began. The State will not so much displace individual enterprise, as substitute for the irresponsible company or "trust" the responsible public corporation. Thirdly, and lastly, be it observed that the arguments used against "government" action, where the government is entirely or mainly in the hands of a ruling class or caste, exercising wisely or unwisely a paternal or "grandmotherly" authority—such arguments lose their force just in proportion as government becomes more and more genuinely the government of the people by the people themselves. The explicit recognition of popular sovereignty tends to abolish the antithesis between "the Man" and "the State." The State becomes, not "I" indeed, but "we." The main reason for desiring more State action is in order to give the individual a greater chance of developing all his activities in a healthy way. The State and the individual are not sides of an antithesis between which we must choose; and it is possible, though, like all great things, difficult, for a democracy to construct a strong and vigorous State, and thereby to foster a strong and vigorous individuality, not selfish nor isolated, but finding it truest welfare in the welfare of the community.

Herbert L. Samuel

THE SOCIAL ETHICS OF LIBERALISM

*Herbert L. Samuel (1870–1963) entered Parliament as a Liberal member in
1902. His valuable work on contemporary liberalism published the same
year, from which the following extracts are chosen, made him one of the
leading spokesmen for the principles and policies that the Liberal party
would endorse as it moved into the twentieth century. Influenced by T. H.
Green at Oxford, Samuel made ethics the first principle of liberalism. In
political terms this meant a program of social reform. The landslide Liberal
victory of 1906 seemed to prove that such a program was palatable to the
voters and was, therefore, a mandate for the government to implement. The
question yet to be answered was whether a bigger and better program of
social reform was a satisfactory solution to the twentieth-century problems
of a mass urban democracy.*

[The opening extract is from Herbert Asquith's introduction to *Liberalism.* As Liberal prime minister, 1908–1916, Asquith attempted to
implement the program of social reform presented below.]

It may seem a truism to say that the Liberal party inscribes among
its permanent watchwords the name of Liberty. That this should
sound like a commonplace is another illustration of the penalties of
success. Freedom of speech, freedom of the press, freedom of association and combination, which we in these latter days have come
to look upon as standing in the same category as the natural right
to light and air, were in point of fact privileges long denied, slowly
attained, and hardly won. But Liberty itself, like so many of the
rallying cries in the secular struggle of parties, is a term which
grows by what it feeds on, and acquires in each generation a new
and larger content. To the early reformers it was a symbol of antagonism and almost of negation; it meant the removal of fetters, the
emancipation both of individuals and of the community from legal
and constitutional disabilities. The abolition of religious tests, the

From Herbert L. Samuel, *Liberalism: An Attempt to State the Principles and Proposals of Contemporary Liberalism in England,* introd. H. H. Asquith (London: G. Rich-
ards, 1902), pp. ix–x, 4, 6, 11, 20–31.

opening up of municipal corporations and the magistracy, the recognition of the legal status of Trades Unions (to take only a few illustrations) were all steps on the road to the peaceful obliteration of feudal and mediæval privileges, which, elsewhere, have been violently submerged beneath the irresistible and often devastating influx of a revolutionary tide. These things no longer admit of argument, but with the growth of experience a more matured opinion has come to recognize that Liberty (in a political sense) is not only a negative but a positive conception. Freedom cannot be predicated, in its true meaning, either of a man or of a society, merely because they are no longer under the compulsion of restraints which have the sanction of positive law. To be really free, they must be able to make the best use of faculty, opportunity, energy, life. It is in this fuller view of the true significance of Liberty that we find the governing impulse in the later developments of Liberalism in the direction of education, temperance, better dwellings, an improved social and industrial environment; everything, in short, that tends to national, communal, and personal efficiency.

*   *   *

If we try to express that [Liberal] doctrine in a single sentence, we shall best formulate it perhaps in these words—That it is the duty of the State to secure to all its members, and all others whom it can influence, the fullest possible opportunity to lead the best life.

When we speak of Progress, we mean by progress the enlargement of this opportunity. When Liberals advocate Self-government, it is because Self-government is regarded as a means towards this end. When they raise the cry of Peace, Retrenchment and Reform, it is because peace, retrenchment and reform are held to be parts of the policy by which the State may fulfil this duty.

*   *   *

That the object of a government should be to help its own subjects, and others whom it can influence, to live well is an idea which is held, of course, not only by Liberals. Socialists and many Conservatives would claim that their policies also have this aim in view.

If the first principle of politics is to be furnished by ethics, it will be clear enough what that first principle must be. Differ as they may in other things, the preachers of every Western religion and the exponents of all the chief schools of modern philosophy agree at least in this one conclusion—the ordinary rule of private morality—that it is the duty of each man to lead, so far as he is able, and to help others to lead, whatever may be held to be the best life. No matter to what faith or school a man may belong, he will not deny the validity of this law. But if this be the duty of the individual, the duty of Society must correspond, must be to aid its own members, and others within its influence, to lead worthy lives; for we cannot imagine a society having an object different from that of the men who compose it. And if such be the duty of Society, it must also be the duty of the State, since the State is nothing else than Society itself organized for purposes of corporate action. Morality teaches, then, that the purpose of the State is to help men, so far as it may be able, to lead their lives in the best way, and a policy which is founded on this rule stands on the firm ground of the moral law. The trunk of the tree of Liberalism is rooted in the soil of ethics. . . .

Our first principle leads clearly and directly to a policy of social reform. Whoever admits that the duty of the State is to secure, so far as it is able, the fullest opportunities to lead the best life, cannot refuse to accept this further proposition, that to lessen the causes of poverty and to lighten its effects are essential parts of a right policy of State action. Liberalism recognizes this; measures to this end are prominent among its objects; and in any attempt to state the aims of Liberalism the proposals of social reform must take the first place.

To many among the fathers of modern Liberalism, government action was anathema. They held, as we hold, that the first and final object of the State is to develop the capacities and raise the standard of living of its citizens; but they held also that the best means towards this object was the self-effacement of the State. Liberty is of supreme importance, and legal regulation is the opposite of liberty. . . .

Contrast this with the measures of social reform that were the distinctive work of the Liberal Government of 1892 to 1895. A striking departure from these principles will be seen.

*   *   *

We naturally seek the causes of the change, and in finding them we shall find also the answer to those who object to it.

In the first place, the State itself has become more competent. Its recent work inspires confidence instead of mistrust. The early Liberals lived under a constitution whose powers had been drawn by means of corruption into the hands of a limited class, and used in defiance of justice to serve the interest of that class. Industry lay at the mercy of a Parliament ignorant of the first laws of political economy, and of a Civil Service and magistracy inefficient for their duties. The State, itself unrepresentative, selfish and unintelligent, had fallen into contempt and had become the aversion of thoughtful men.

Now democracy has been substituted for aristocracy as the root principle of the constitution. Court influence and the grosser kinds of corruption have disappeared. Efficient local authorities and an expert Civil Service have been created. The whole machinery of government has been vastly changed and improved. A new system has been called into being—mainly through the efforts of the early Liberals themselves—and the State of to-day is held worthy to be the agent of the community in many affairs for which the State of yesterday was clearly incompetent.

In the second place, while these experiments in legislation were modifying opinion by their success, the social conscience was becoming more fully awake to the urgent need of improvement, and the inability of the *laissez faire* policy to bring it about was gradually becoming more plain.

The growing wealth of the commercial and landed classes had thrown the facts of poverty into sharper relief. Carlyle and Ruskin by their passionate denunciations, Dickens and George Eliot by their appeals to sentiment, and a crowd of lesser writers following the same paths, contributed to make the nation realize that here was a cause of shame. And the working-classes themselves, organized in Trade Unions and at last enfranchised, were able to command the attention which had been denied to their silent suffering.

The widespread eagerness for social progress which was so marked a feature of the nineteenth century, and particularly of the latter half of it, rebelled against the slow and doubtful methods of *laissez faire*. The restrictive laws, which the individualists declared to be the chief barriers to improvement, had been repealed. But the condition of the poorer classes seemed in many respects to be hardly at all the better. A stern experience was fast convincing the people that "the free play of enlightened self-interest," on which the Manchester School wholly relied to bring progress, was a force insufficient for the needs of the case; that the "self-reliance and enterprise" of the working-classes were faced by barriers too formidable to be conquered without help. . . .

Another influence was also at work. So far as questions of labour regulation were concerned, there was arising a new doctrine of the true meaning and the best guarantees of liberty. It was urged that legal restrictions might after all be made to extend rather than to limit freedom and would often stop more compulsion than they imposed.

Because the law does not interfere with his actions a man is not necessarily free. There is economic restriction as well as legal restriction. If the tramway conductor agrees to serve twelve hours a day for thirteen days out of fourteen, we cannot say that, because no law compels him, he does this of his own choice. The industrial system irresistibly bends to its will all who form part of it; the workman must submit to the customs of his trade and workshop under penalty of dismissal; liberty to "go elsewhere" is an empty privilege when the conditions are everywhere the same.

Therefore, it was argued, the State must intervene in the interest of liberty itself. As the law prohibiting duelling provided the only means of escape from an oppressive social custom and enlarged freedom by means of restrictions, so labour legislation is often the only means of rescue for those who are subject to oppressive industrial customs.

Three causes, then, combined to convert Liberalism from the principle of State abstention. . . . It was seen that the State had become more efficient and its legislation more competent, and laws of regulation were found by experiment neither to lessen prosperity nor to weaken self-reliance in the manner foretold. It was realized that the conditions of society were in many respects so bad that to tolerate them longer was impossible, and that the *laissez faire* policy was not likely to bring the cure. And it was realized that extensions of law need not imply diminutions of freedom, but on the contrary would often enlarge freedom.

*   *   *

There is a line, then between the sphere of State action and the sphere of private action. But can this line be described in words? Search as we may, we shall never find a single formula which will cover all cases of legitimate State action and exclude all cases of illegitimate State action. The engineer might as well try to define by a general statement the boundaries between the sphere of machine labour and the sphere of hand labour, as the politician try to define the boundaries between the province of the State and the province of private action. The only acceptable rule is that of Jevons: "The State is justified in passing any law, or in doing any single act, which, without ulterior consequences, adds to the sum-total of human happiness." And this is far too indefinite a rule to be of any use whatever as a guide in practical politics.

Yet there are certain vague general principles, rarely disputed, which must always influence the statesman.

Only in extreme cases, such as the case of the unhealthy trades, may the State use coercion except as a means of directly enlarging liberty. The law should not do for the individual that which he might do for himself without undue delay or an undue expenditure of energy; for otherwise self-reliance would be weakened. Distress must not be relieved in such a way as to encourage thriftlessness and burden the industrious for the benefit of the wilfully idle or vicious. If industry is touched it must be with a cautious hand, and so as not to lessen the volume of national trade. The laws must not discriminate between individuals. They must be such as can be practically enforced. They must not be of a kind to cause revolutionary disturbance. Examine the various measures which are now advocated by Liberals, and it will be found that it is these commonplace rules that chiefly decide their character. These vaguely fix the practical limits of State interference.

From time to time the State undertakes fresh duties. As new wants arise, and as government becomes more efficient, the province of State action is gradually enlarged. For this reason the

Liberal programme of to-day is very different from that of a century ago. It makes no claim to finality. Liberalism, indeed, is no stereotyped collection of fixed proposals. It is a living force that applies itself in turn to all the changing phases of national life, in ways conditioned by the character and the customs of the people. As times alter, the proposals of Liberalism must alter as well.

David Lloyd George

SOCIAL WELFARE: A RIGHT NOT A PRIVILEGE

A Nonconformist Welshman in politics without the conventional credentials, David Lloyd George (1863–1945) cultivated the masses at the expense of the traditional power structure. The new liberalism, for him, meant better conditions for the poor and more taxes for the rich. In 1908–1909 as head of the treasury and prime mover in the Liberal cabinet for social reform, he was in a unique position both to raise taxes and to reduce poverty. The budget fight that ensued between the Commons and the Lords changed the face of British politics. That conflict was given a provocative and, at times, demagogic dimension by Lloyd George's speeches against the landed interests. The following extracts capture the capacity of the "Welsh Wizard" to draw striking poetic and Biblical word pictures, which in their day had the power to move crowds. In 1916 Lloyd George became the last Liberal prime minister.

Speech at Swansea, October 1, 1908

What is the work still waiting the Liberal Party in this country? It is to establish complete religious equality in our institutions. There is no religious equality so long as men of capacity and character are debarred from competing for teacherships in 14,000 State schools because they cannot conscientiously conform to the doctrines of some dominant sect. There is no religious equality as long as one

From David Lloyd George, *Better Times* (London: Hodder and Stoughton, 1910), pp. 49–54, 173–175. Reprinted by permission of The First Beaverbrook Foundation.

sect whose dogmas, in Wales at any rate, are repudiated by the vast majority of the people, is able to pose as the official exponent of the faith of the Welsh people, and to enjoy all the privileges, emoluments, and endowments attached to that position. I place the establishment of complete religious equality in the forefront, because it lies in the domain of conscience . . . and nothing can save a people afflicted by such institutions from the spirit of bondage but an incessant protest against them . . . .

The same observations apply to the question of civil equality. We have not yet attained it in this country—far from it. You will not have established it in this land until the child of the poorest parent shall have the same opportunity for receiving the best education as the child of the richest . . . . It will never be established so long as you have five hundred men nominated by the lottery of birth to exercise the right of thwarting the wishes of the majority of forty millions of their countrymen in the determination of the best way of governing the country. I hope no prospect of a temporary material advantage will blind the people of this country to the permanent good for them of vindicating in the laws and institutions of the land these great principles, which lie at the root of freedom and good government for the people.

On the other hand, I think there is a danger that Liberals may imagine that their task begins and ends there. If they do so, then they will not accomplish even that task.

British Liberalism is not going to repeat the fate of Continental Liberalism. The fate of Continental Liberalism should warn them of that danger. It has been swept on one side before it had well begun its work, because it refused to adapt itself to new conditions. The Liberalism of the Continent concerned itself exclusively with mending and perfecting the machinery which was to grind corn for the people. It forgot that the people had to live whilst the process was going on, and people saw their lives pass away without anything being accomplished. British Liberalism has been better advised. It has not abandoned the traditional ambition of the Liberal Party to establish freedom and equality; but side by side with this effort it promotes measures for ameliorating the conditions of life for the multitude.

The old Liberals in this country used the natural discontent of the people with the poverty and precariousness of the means of subsistence as a motive power to win for them a better, more influential, and more honourable status in the citizenship of their native land. The new Liberalism, while pursuing this great political ideal with unflinching energy, devotes a part of its endeavour also to the removing of the immediate causes of discontent. It is true that men cannot live by bread alone. It is equally true that a man cannot live without bread. . . . It is a recognition of that elemental fact that has promoted legislation like the Old Age Pensions Act. It is but the beginning of things. . . . Poverty is the result of a man's own misconduct or misfortune. In so far as he brings it on himself, the State cannot accomplish much. It can do something to protect him. In so far as poverty is due to circumstances over which the man has no control, then the State should step in to the very utmost limit of its resources, and save the man from the physical and mental torture involved in extreme penury. . . . The aged we have dealt with during the present Session. We are still confronted with the more gigantic task of dealing with the rest—the sick, the infirm, the unemployed, the widows, and the orphans. No country can lay any real claim to civilisation that allows them to starve. Starvation is a punishment that society has ceased to inflict for centuries on its worst criminals, and at its most barbarous stage humanity never starved the children of the criminal. . . . Is it just, is it fair, is it humane, to let them suffer privation? I do not think the better-off classes, whose comfort is assured, realise the sufferings of the unemployed workmen. What is poverty? Have you felt it yourselves? If not, you ought to thank God for having been spared its sufferings and temptations. Have you ever seen others enduring it? Then pray God to forgive you if you have not done your best to alleviate it. By poverty I mean real poverty, not the cutting down of your establishment, not the limitation of your luxuries. I mean the poverty of the man who does not know how long he can keep a roof over his head, and where he will turn to find a meal for the pinched and hungry little children who look to him for sustenance and protection. That is what unemployment means.

*   *   *

Speech at Newcastle, October 9, 1909

Well, now, we are going to send the Bill [the Finance Bill, the Lloyd George Budget of 1909] up—all the taxes or none. What will the Lords do? I tell you frankly it is a matter which concerns them far more than it concerns us . . . .

Who talks about altering or meddling with the Constitution? The Constitutional party—the great Constitutional party. As long as the Constitution gave rank and possession and power to the Lords it was not to be interfered with. As long as it secured even their sports from intrusion and made interference with them a crime; as long as the Constitution enforced royalties and ground rents and fees and premiums and fines, and all the black retinue of exaction; as long as it showered writs and summonses and injunctions and distresses and warrants to enforce them, then the Constitution was inviolate. It was something that was put in the same category as religion, that no man should touch with rude hands, something that the chivalry of the nation ought to range itself in defence of. But the moment the Constitution looks round; the moment the Constitution begins to discover that there are millions of people ouside park gates who need attention, then the Constitution is to be torn to pieces.

Let them realise what they are doing. They are forcing a revolution, and they will get it. The Lords may decree a revolution, but the people will direct it. If they begin, issues will be raised that they little dream of. Questions will be asked which are now whispered in humble voices, and answers will be demanded then with authority. The question will be asked whether five hundred men, ordinary men chosen accidentally from among the unemployed, should override the judgement of millions of people who are engaged in the industry which makes the wealth of the country.

That is one question. Another will be, Who ordained that a few should have the land of Britain as a perquisite? Who made ten thousand people owners of the soil, and the rest of us trespassers in the land of our birth? Who is it who is responsible for the scheme of things whereby one man is engaged through life in grinding labour to win a bare and precarious subsistence for himself, and when at the end of his days, he claims at the hands of the community he served a poor pension of eight pence a day, he can only get it through a revolution; and another man who does not toil receives every hour of the day, every hour of the night while he slumbers, more than his poor neighbour receives in a whole year of toil? Where did the table of that law come from? Whose finger inscribed it? These are the questions that will be asked.

John A. Hobson
ORGANIC NATURE OF THE STATE

John A. Hobson (1858–1940) was recognized as a leading critic of orthodox economic doctrines, which he attacked largely from a sociological position. In many ways he anticipated the economic views later associated with John Maynard Keynes. Hobson's organic view of social reconstruction offered liberalism a new interpretation of private enterprise. No longer was property an inherent individual right, since the community, as well as the individual, was a producer of values. Hobson's doctrine of the general will has obvious implications for democracy and Nonconformity. A comparison of Hobson and Mill on these questions is recommended to the reader. If Hobson's economic and sociological reformulations moved liberalism toward a collectivist ideology, the more traditional liberal viewpoint on imperialism is forcefully restated in Hobson's classic Imperialism, A Study *(1902).*

For over a quarter of a century Liberalism has wandered in this valley of indecision, halting, weak, vacillating, divided, and concessive. Not gaining ground, it yielded it. . . .

It is this disbelief in the spiritual strength of Liberalism, thus derived, that explains why Conservatism, defeated in its assault upon the fortress of Free Trade, rallies again to a more formidable attack upon the principle of popular representative government.

To many Liberals this movement of the Lords seems wanton folly. But it is not. It is a half-conscious recognition of the intrinsic or essential nature of the new Liberalism, which during the last few

From John A. Hobson, *The Crisis of Liberalism: New Issues of Democracy* (London: P. S. King and Son, 1909), pp. viii–xi, xiv, 3–4, 6, 74–78, 92–95, 113. Reprinted by permission of Staples Press Ltd.

years has moved forward quickly from the shadowy background of the political stage towards actuality in statecraft. The reason, a quite sufficient one, why Conservatives have decided to stake the very constitution in the hazard of the present fight, is that they recognise in the New Liberalism, to which they think the Government has been reluctantly committed by Mr. George and Mr. Churchill, the beginnings of an unceasing and an enlarging attack upon the system of private property and private industrial enterprise. Actuated rather by a true instinct of self-defence than by a fully reasoned policy, they have decided to fight this New Liberalism before it has captured the firm adhesion of the party and the imagination of the people. . . .

Will Liberalism, reformed and dedicated to this new, enlarged, and positive task of realising liberty, carry its adherents with unbroken ranks with persistent vigour along this march of social progress?

The real crisis of Liberalism lies here, not in the immediate capacity to resist the insolent encroachment of the unrepresentative House, but in the intellectual and moral ability to accept and execute a positive progressive policy which involves a new conception of the functions of the State.

It is true that no sudden reversal of policy is required: the old individualism has long since been replaced by various enlargements of public activity. But hitherto these interferences and novel functions of the State have been mostly unconnected actions of an opportunist character: no avowed principle or system has underlain them. This opportunism, this studied disavowal of ulterior meaning, disarmed much opposition in the ranks of Liberalism: so long as "Socialistic" measures were shown as single moves in a party game, played by both sides, little offence was caused.

* * *

Our crisis consists in the substitution of an organic for an opportunist policy, the adoption of a vigorous, definite, positive policy of social reconstruction, involving important modifications in the legal and economic institutions of private property and private industry. For any faithful analysis of our existing economic system will show that nothing less can fulfil the demand, which Mr.

Churchill has expressed, that "property—be associated in the minds of the mass of the people with ideas of reason and justice."

No one who follows the new crystallisation of Liberal policy, as displayed in the anti-destitution and insurance proposals of the Government, to which substance is already given in Old Age Pensions, Wages Boards, and Labour Exchanges, in the public provision for the development of our natural resources, in the Small Holdings and Town Planning policy, and in the financial claims of the State to participation in "unearned increments," can fail to recognise a coherency of purpose, an organic plan of social progress, which implies a new consciousness of Liberal statecraft.

The full implications of this movement may not be clearly grasped, but Liberalism is now formally committed to a task which certainly involves a new conception of the State in its relation to the individual life and to private enterprise. That conception is not Socialism, in any accredited meaning of that term, though implying a considerable amount of increased public ownership and control of industry. From the standpoint which best presents its continuity with earlier Liberalism, it appears as a fuller appreciation and realisation of individual liberty contained in the provision of equal opportunities for self-development. But to this individual standpoint must be joined a just apprehension of the social, viz., the insistence that these claims or rights of self-development be adjusted to the sovereignty of social welfare.

*　　*　　*

The whole conception of the State disclosed by these new issues, as an instrument for the active adaptation of the economic and moral environment to the new needs of individual and social life, by securing full opportunities of self-development and social service for all citizens, was foreign to the Liberalism of the last generation. Now, in England, as elsewhere, these positive, constructive, and primarily economic proposals are clamouring for consideration. The old *laissez-faire* Liberalism is dead. Its early demise might indeed have been predicted from the time when Cobden recognised the necessity of "freeing" the land of England as he had helped to "free" her trade. For the effective liberation of the land, as we now perceive, involves large permanent measures of public control, and brings in its wake a long series of further enlargements of State activity in transport, credit, housing, and other matters. The slow education which the land question has conducted upon the nature of monopoly and socially-created values, was bound in time to bear fruit in a growing recognition of similar elements of monopoly and social values inherent not only in liquor licences and other legalised monopolies but everywhere throughout the industrial system where competition is impeded or estopped. So, quite apart from any theoretic Socialism, there has been formed in the public mind a firm conviction that, wherever these obstructions to economic liberty are found, the State must exert its powers, either to restore free competition, or, where that is impracticable or unwise, to substitute a public monopoly in which all share for a private monopoly the profits of which pass to a favoured few.

The New Liberalism has absorbed this teaching and is preparing to put it into practice.

* * *

In England, as elsewhere where a fervid passion of social reform has arisen, reformers have been indignant at the suggestion that it may be more economical to postpone the immediate realisation of their proposals until they have removed obstructions in electoral and legislative institutions. They are tired, they say, of tinkering with political machinery; a popular franchise already exists, the people can now get their will if they stand together and shout loud enough. Now all who have made a close study of the actual operation of the so-called democratic machinery, in Europe or in America, perceive that this view is false. Ostrogorski's study of the mechanics of the party system in the United States and in Great Britain shows to what perilous abuses the forms of representative government are exposed, and how feebly and irregularly the real spirit of democracy pulses through them. The defects of representation are not the same in the two countries. In America it is the "spoils," corrupting the party system from the national convention down to the ward "primary," and the rigours of a written constitution which preclude amendment. In England it is the refusal to give completeness to the representative forms and to provide democratic safeguards against abuses of them.

* * *

This Spirit of the Hive or of the Herd is a true spirit of Society, a single unity of purpose in the community. Those who would cut the Gordian knot of this problem by saying that individuals alone are ends, and that Society is nothing but a means to these ends, will find it difficult to make their theory square with the facts of natural history in which the individual always appears as a means to the collective end of the maintenance of the race.

Those who would distinguish in kind this social or gregarious instinct of the lower animals from the individual reasonable consciousness in man have no warrant for their distinction. For there is ample testimony that the mind of man, in its feeling, its thinking, its will, is not the separate thing it seems at first to be.

Setting aside all the dubious and difficult evidence of direct intentional impact of one mind upon another by telepathy, and other similar methods, the growth and operations of a common mind or purpose formed by the direct interaction of many individual minds cannot seriously be questioned.

Even the fortuitous concourse of a crowd shows this: a mob in the streets of Paris or of London exhibits a character and a behaviour which is uniform, is dominated for the time being by a single feeling or idea, and differs widely from the known character and behaviour of its component members. Look at the effect of an orator upon a crowd, the power of a sudden panic, the contagion of some quick impulse to action; it is quite evident that the barriers which commonly encase the individual mind have given way, that the private judgment is inhibited, and that for a time a mob-mind has been set up in its stead, in which the reasoning faculties are almost suspended, and in which the passions of animal ferocity, generosity, credulity, self-sacrifice, malignity, and courage express themselves unrestrained.

A great personality, a great religious or political idea, a mere mis-statement invented by a lying Press, may weld into a common desire, a common will, the minds of a whole nation: the result is not intelligible as the added action of the same idea acting on so many separate minds: it is the inter-action of these minds growing by stronger social sympathy into fusion that is the real phenomenon. . . .

This is the doctrine of the general will, as I understand it, which Rousseau, among moderns, was the first clearly to enumerate, which has been developed on its political side by Hegel and his followers, and which in English finds its most masterly expression in Mr. Bosanquet's work, *The Philosophical Theory of the State.*

To the common-sense objector who says, "A nation does not think, a nation does not feel, it is individuals who do these things," I would reply that if you could talk with a "cell" of the human body it would tell you it is not *we* who think and feel, but the separate cells, each of which is conscious in itself of such processes, but from the nature of the case is not and cannot be conscious of the feeling and thinking which goes on in the organism as a whole.

A nation does feel, and think, not so fully, so wholesomely, so happily as it should and will, when the process of forming a social organism has gone further, but within the limits of such conscious unity as it has attained . . . .

The practical value of this thought consists in the material it yields for restating the doctrine of Democracy. It is quite evident that the conception of Society as a moral organism negates the old democratic idea of political equality based on the notion that every member of a political society had an inherent right to the same power as every other in determining the action of Society. The idea of natural individual rights as the basis of Democracy disappears. Take, for instance, the formula of "No taxation without representation." From the standpoint of individualist Democracy this is understood to imply that, when the State takes away some of my property by taxing me, I have some right to earmark the tax I pay and to say what shall be done with it, or with a corresponding portion of the public funds afterwards. Now a clear grasp of Society as an economic organism completely explodes the notion of property as an inherent individual right, for it shows that no individual can make or appropriate anything of value without the direct continuous assistance of Society. So the idea of Society as a political organism insists that the general will and wisdom of the Society, as embodied in the State, shall determine the best social use of all the social property taken by taxation, without admitting any inherent right of interference on the part of the taxpayer. This does not, indeed, imply that "No taxation without representation," is an unsound maxim of government: on the contrary, it may be, and I think is, strongly advisable that those from whom taxes are levied shall watch and check the use which Government may make of them: but the worth of this practice is defensible not on grounds of individual right but of general expediency, because persons who have paid a tax will be found to be better guardians of the public purse than those who have not paid it.

*   *   *

The negative conception of Liberalism, as a definite mission for the removal of certain political and economic shackles upon personal liberty, is not merely philosophically defective, but historically false. The Liberals of this country as a party never committed themselves either to the theory or the policy of this narrow *laissez-faire* individualism; they never conceived liberty as something limited in quantity, or purely negative in character. But it is true that they tended to lay an excessive emphasis upon the aspect of liberty which consists in absence of restraint, as compared with the other aspect which consists in presence of opportunity; and it is this tendency, still lingering in the mind of the Liberal Party, that to-day checks its energy and blurs its vision. A more constructive and a more evolutionary idea of liberty is needed to give the requisite *élan de vie* to the movement; and every cause of liberation, individual, class, sex, and national, must be recharged with the fresh enthusiasm of this fuller faith.

Liberalism will probably retain its distinction from Socialism, in taking for its chief test of policy the freedom of the individual citizen rather than the strength of the State, though the antagonism of the two standpoints may tend to disappear in the light of progressive experience. But it will justify itself by two great enlargements of its liberative functions. In seeking to realise liberty for the individual citizen as "equality of opportunity," it will recognise that, as the area and nature of opportunities are continually shifting, so the old limited conception of the task of Liberalism must always advance. Each generation of Liberals will be required to translate a new set of needs and aspirations into facts. It is because we have fallen so far short of due performance of this task that our Liberalism shows signs of enfeeblement. We must fearlessly face as our first, though not our only question, What is a free Englishman to-day? If we answer this question faithfully, we shall recognise that it comprises many elements of real liberty and opportunity which have not been won for the people as a whole. Is a man free who has not equal opportunity with his fellows of such access to all material and moral means of personal development and work as shall contribute to his own welfare and that of his society? Such equal opportunity at least implies an equal access to the use of his native land as a workplace and a home, such mobility as will enable him to dispose of his personal energies to the best advantage, easy access to that factor of capital or credit which modern industry recognises as essential to economic independence, and to whatever new form of industrial power, electric or other, may be needed to co-operate with human efforts. A man is not really free for purposes of self-development in life and work who is not adequately provided in all these respects, and no small part of constructive Liberalism must be devoted to the attainment of these equal opportunities.

Finally, though Liberals must ever insist that each enlargement of the authority and functions of the State must justify itself as an enlargement of personal liberty, interfering with individuals only in order to set free new and larger opportunities, there need remain in Liberalism no relics of that positive hostility to public methods of co-operation which crippled the old Radicalism. When Society is confronted, as it sometimes will be, by a breakdown of competition and a choice between private monopoly and public enterprise, no theoretic objections to the State can be permitted to militate against public safety. Just in proportion as education guides, enriches, and enlightens the will of the people, and gives spiritual substance and intellectual power to democracy, the presumption which still holds against the adequacy of public as compared with private co-operation will be weakened, and Liberalism will come more definitely to concern itself with the liberation and utilisation of the faculties and potencies of a nation and a municipality, as well as with those of individuals and voluntary groups of citizens. It surely belongs to Liberalism to think thus liberally about its mission and its modes of progressive achievement. Not, however, of fulfilment. For it is this illimitable character of Liberalism, based on the infinitude of the possibilities of human life, in its individual and social aspects, which affords that vision without which not only a people but a party perishes. . . .

It is true that the attainment of this practical equalisation of opportunities involves a larger use of the State and legislation than Liberals of an older school recognised as necessary or desirable. But the needs of our day are different from theirs, and the modern State is a different instrument. There is nothing in Liberalism to preclude a self-governing people from using the instrument of self-government for any of the measures I have named: on the contrary, to refuse to do so is to furnish the mere forms of liberty and to deny the substance. Moreover, there is not one of these great positive liberties that has not been acknowledged and in large part secured for the people by some advanced State in Europe or in our colonies. Free land, free travel, free power, free credit, security, justice, and education, no man is "free" for the full purposes of civilised life to-day unless he has all these liberties.

*   *   *

The future of Liberalism depends upon the willingness and the ability of its professed adherents to confront courageously and hopefully these large demands for the restatement of the Liberal creed, and its realisation in the new economic and moral world opening out before us.

Leonard T. Hobhouse
LIBERAL SOCIALISM

Leonard T. Hobhouse (1864–1929) wrote the first of his sixteen books as a tutor at Corpus Christi College, Oxford, in 1893. Four years later he joined the editorial staff of the Manchester Guardian, *only to return to academic life as the first professor of sociology at the University of London. Aiming at a harmonious society that would provide the greatest potentiality for human growth, he envisioned a liberal socialism evolving out of democratic liberalism. Such growth demanded state planning. If society is mobilized for war*

From Leonard T. Hobhouse, *Liberalism* (New York: Oxford University Press, 1964), pp. 66–73, 76–78, 82–84, 87, 90–91, 107–110, 115–116, 126. Reprinted by permission of the Clarendon Press, Oxford.

and destruction, why not for positive social ends such as full employment or care for the aged? His political creed is expounded in the following passages from Liberalism *(1911), in which he endeavored in England, as John Dewey attempted in the United States, to preserve within a liberal welfare state the traditional accent on individual liberty.*

The foundation of liberty is the idea of growth. Life is learning, but whether in theory or practice what a man genuinely learns is what he absorbs, and what he absorbs depends on the energy which he himself puts forth in response to his surroundings. Thus, to come at once to the real crux, the question of moral discipline, it is of course possible to reduce a man to order and prevent him from being a nuisance to his neighbours by arbitrary control and harsh punishment. This may be to the comfort of the neighbours, as is admitted, but regarded as a moral discipline it is a contradiction in terms. It is doing less than nothing for the character of the man himself. It is merely crushing him, and unless his will is killed the effect will be seen if ever the superincumbent pressure is by chance removed. It is also possible, though it takes a much higher skill, to teach the same man to discipline himself, and this is to foster the development of will, of personality, of self-control, or whatever we please to call that central harmonizing power which makes us capable of directing our own lives. Liberalism is the belief that society can safely be founded on this self-directing power of personality, that it is only on this foundation that a true community can be built, and that so established its foundations are so deep and so wide that there is no limit that we can place to the extent of the building. Liberty then becomes not so much a right of the individual as a necessity of society. It rests not on the claim of A to be let alone by B, but on the duty of B to treat A as a rational being. It is not right to let crime alone or to let error alone, but it is imperative to treat the criminal or the mistaken or the ignorant as beings capable of right and truth, and to lead them on instead of merely beating them down. The rule of liberty is just the application of rational method. It is the opening of the door to the appeal of reason, of imagination, of social feeling; and except through the responses to this appeal there is no assured progress of society.

Now, I am not contending that these principles are free from difficulty in application. At many points they suggest difficulties both in theory and in practice. . . . Nor, again, am I contending that freedom is the universal solvent, or the idea of liberty the sole foundation on which a true social philosophy can be based. On the contrary, freedom is only one side of social life. Mutual aid is not less important than mutual forbearance, the theory of collective action no less fundamental than the theory of personal freedom.

. . . Beginning with the right of the individual, and the antithesis between personal freedom and social control, we have been led on to a point at which we regard liberty as primarily a matter of social interest, as something flowing from the necessities of continuous advance in those regions of truth and of ethics which constitute the matters of highest social concern. At the same time, we have come to look for the effect of liberty in the firmer establishment of social solidarity, as the only foundation on which such solidarity can securely rest. We have, in fact, arrived by a path of our own at that which is ordinarily described as the organic conception of the relation between the individual and society—a conception towards which Mill worked through his career, and which forms the starting-point of T. H. Green's philosophy alike in ethics and in politics.

The term organic is so much used and abused that it is best to state simply what it means. A thing is called organic when it is made up of parts which are quite distinct from one another, but which are destroyed or vitally altered when they are removed from the whole. Thus, the human body is organic because its life depends on the functions performed by many organs, while each of these organs depends in turn on the life of the body, perishing and decomposing if removed therefrom. Now, the organic view of society is equally simple. It means that, while the life of society is nothing but the life of individuals as they act one upon another, the life of the individual in turn would be something utterly different if he could be separated from society. A great deal of him would not exist at all. . . .

The argument might seem to make the individual too subservient to society. But this is to forget the other side of the original supposition. Society consists wholly of persons. It has no distinct personality separate from and superior to those of its members. It has, indeed, a certain collective life and character. The British nation is a unity with a life of its own. But the unity is constituted by certain ties that bind together all British subjects, which ties are in the last resort feelings and ideas, sentiments of patriotism, of kinship, a common pride, and a thousand more subtle sentiments that bind together men who speak a common language, have behind them a common history, and understand one another as they can understand no one else. The British nation is not a mysterious entity over and above the forty odd millions of living souls who dwell together under a common law. Its life is their life, its well-being or ill-fortune their well-being or ill-fortune. Thus, the common good to which each man's rights are subordinate is a good in which each man has a share. This share consists in realizing his capacities of feeling, of loving, of mental and physical energy, and in realizing these he plays his part in the social life, or, in Green's phrase, he finds his own good in the common good.

Now, this phrase, it must be admitted, involves a certain assumption, which may be regarded as the fundamental postulate of the organic view of society. It implies that such a fulfilment or full development of personality is practically possible not for one man only but for all members of a community. There must be a line of development open along which each can move in harmony with others. Harmony in the full sense would involve not merely absence of conflict but actual support. There must be for each, then, possibilities of development such as not merely to permit but actively to further the development of others. Now, the older economists conceived a natural harmony, such that the intersts of each would, if properly understood and unchecked by outside interference, inevitably lead him in courses profitable to others and to society at large. We saw that this assumption was too optimistic. The conception which we have now reached does not assume so much. It postulates, not that there is an actually existing harmony requiring nothing but prudence and coolness of judgment for its effective operation, but only that there is a possible ethical harmony, to which, partly by discipline, partly by the improvement of the conditions of life, men might attain, and that in such attainment lies the social ideal. To attempt the systematic proof of this postulate would take us into the field of philosophical first principles. It is the point at which the philosophy of politics comes into contact with that of ethics, It must suffice to say here that, just as the endeavour to establish coherent system in the world of thought is the characteristic of the rational impulse which lies at the root of science and philosophy, so the impulse to establish harmony in the world of feeling and action—a harmony which must include all those who think and feel—is of the essence of the rational impulse in the world of practice. To move towards harmony is the persistent impulse of the rational being, even if the goal lies always beyond the reach of accomplished effort.

These principles may appear very abstract, remote from practical life, and valueless for concrete teaching, But this remoteness is of the nature of first principles when taken without the connecting links that bind them to the details of experience. To find some of these links let us take up again our old Liberal principles, and see how they look in the light of the organic, or, as we may now call it, the harmonic conception. We shall readily see, to begin with, that the old idea of equality has its place, For the common good includes every individual. It is founded on personality, and postulates free scope for the development of personality in each member of the community. This is the foundation not only of equal rights before the law, but also of what is called equality of opportunity. It does not necessarily imply actual equality of treatment for all persons any more than it implies original equality of powers. It does, I think, imply that whatever inequality of actual treatment, of income, rank, office, consideration, there be in a good social system, it would rest, not on the interest of the favoured individual as such, but on the common good. If the existence of millionaires on the one hand and of paupers on the other is just, it must be because such contrasts are the result of an economic system which upon the whole works out for the common good, the good of the pauper being included therein as well as the good of the millionaire; that is to say, that when we have well weighed the good and the evil of all parties concerned we can find no alternative open to us which could do better for the good of all. . . .

If we turn from equality to liberty, the general lines of argument have already been indicated. . . . It need only be repeated here that on the harmonic principle the fundamental importance of liberty rests on the nature of the "good" itself, and that whether we are thinking of the good of society or the good of the individual. The good is something attained by the development of the basal factors of personality, a development proceeding by the widening of ideas, the awakening of the imagination, the play of affection and passion, the strengthening and extension of rational control. As it is the development of these factors in each human being that makes his life worth having, so it is their harmonious interaction, the response of each to each, that makes of society a living whole. Liberty so interpreted cannot, as we have seen, dispense with restraint; restraint, however, is not an end but a means to an end, and one of the principal elements in that end is the enlargement of liberty.

. . . The heart of Liberalism is the understanding that progress is not a matter of mechanical contrivance, but of the liberation of living spiritual energy. Good mechanism is that which provides the channels wherein such energy can flow unimpeded, unobstructed by its own exuberance of output, vivifying the social structure, expanding and ennobling the life of mind.

* * *

For the moment we have to deal only with those actions of State which compel all citizens, or all whom they concern, to fall in with them and allow of no divergence. This kind of coercion tends to increase. Is its extension necessarily an encroachment upon liberty, or are the elements of value secured by collective control distinct from the elements of value secured by individual choice, so that within due limits each may develop side by side?

We have already declined to solve the problem by applying Mill's distinction between self-regarding and other-regarding actions, first because there are no actions which may not directly or indirectly affect others, secondly because even if there were they would not cease to be matter of concern to others. The common good includes the good of every member of the community, and the injury which a man inflicts upon himself is matter of common concern, even apart from any ulterior effect upon others. If we refrain from coercing a man for his own good, it is not because his good is indifferent to us, but because it cannot be furthered by coercion . . . .

Where, then, is the sphere of compulsion, and what is its value? The reply is that compulsion is of value where outward conformity is of value, and this may be in any case where the nonconformity of one wrecks the purpose of others. We have already remarked that liberty itself only rests upon restraint. Thus a religious body is not, properly speaking, free to march in procession through the streets unless people of a different religion are restrained from pelting the procession with stones and pursuing it with insolence. We restrain them from disorder not to teach them the genuine spirit of religion, which they will not learn in the police court, but to secure to the other party the right of worship unmolested. The enforced restraint has its value in the action that it sets free. But we may not only restrain one man from obstructing another—and the extent to which we do this is the measure of the freedom that we maintain—but we may also restrain him from obstructing the general will; and this we have to do whenever uniformity is necessary to the end which the general will has in view. . . .

It appears, then, that the true distinction is not between self-regarding and other-regarding actions, but between coercive and non-coercive actions. The function of State coercion is to override individual coercion, and, of course, coercion exercised by any association of individuals within the State. It is by this means that it maintains liberty of expression, security of person and property, genuine freedom of contract, the rights of public meeting and association, and finally its own power to carry out common objects undefeated by the recalcitrance of individual members. Undoubtedly it endows both individuals and associations with powers as well as with rights. But over these powers it must exercise supervision in the interests of equal justice. Just as compulsion failed in the sphere of liberty, the sphere of spiritual growth, so liberty fails in the external order wherever, by the mere absence of supervisory restriction, men are able directly or indirectly to put constraint on one another. This is why there is no intrinsic and inevitable conflict between liberty and compulsion, but at bottom a mutual need. The object of compulsion is to secure the most favourable external conditions of inward growth and happiness so far as these conditions depend on combined action and uniform observance. The sphere of liberty is the sphere of growth itself. There is no true opposition between liberty as such and control as such, for every liberty rests on a corresponding act of control.

*   *   *

So far we have been considering what the State compels the individual to do. If we pass to the question what the State is to do for the individual, a different but parallel question arises, and we have to note a corresponding movement of opinion. If the State does for the individual what he ought to do for himself what will be the effect on character, initiative, enterprise? It is a question now not of freedom, but of responsibility, and it is one that has caused many searchings of heart, and in respect of which opinion has undergone a remarkable change. Thus, in relation to poverty the older view was that the first thing needful was self-help. It was the business of every man to provide for himself and his family. If, indeed, he utterly failed, neither he nor they could be left to starve, and there was the Poor Law machinery to deal with his case. But the aim of every sincere friend of the poor must be to keep them away from the Poor Law machine. Experience of the forty years before 1834 had taught us what came of free resort to public funds by way of subvention to inadequate wages. It meant simply that the standard of remuneration was lowered in proportion as men could rely on public aid to make good the deficiency, while at the same time the incentives to independent labour were weakened when the pauper stood on an equal footing with the hard-working man. In general, if the attempt was made to substitute for personal effort the help of others, the result would only sap individual initiative and in the end bring down the rate of industrial remuneration. It was thought, for example—and this very point was urged against proposals for Old Age Pensions—that if any of the objects for which a man will, if possible, provide were removed from the scope of his own activity, he would in consequence be content with proportionally lower wages; if the employer was to compensate him for accident, he would fail to make provision for accidents on his own account; if his children were fed by the ratepayers, he would not earn the money wherewith to feed them. . . .

We said above that it was the function of the State to secure the conditions upon which mind and character may develop themselves. Similarly we may say now that the function of the State is to secure conditions upon which its citizens are able to win by their own efforts all that is necessary to a full civic efficiency. It is not for the State to feed, house, or clothe them. It is for the State to take care that the economic conditions are such that the normal man who is not defective in mind or body or will can by useful labour feed, house, and clothe himself and his family. The "right to work" and the right to a "living wage" are just as valid as the rights of person or property. That is to say, they are integral conditions of a good social order. A society in which a single honest man of normal capacity is definitely unable to find the means of maintaining himself by useful work is to that extent suffering from malorganization. There is somewhere a defect in the social system, a hitch in the economic machine. Now, the individual workman cannot put the machine straight. He is the last person to have any say in the control of the market. It is not his fault if there is over-production in his industry, or if a new and cheaper process has been introduced which makes his particular skill, perhaps the product of years of application, a drug in the market. He does not direct or regulate industry. He is not responsible for its ups and downs, but he has to pay for them. That is why it is not charity but justice for which he is asking.

*   *   *

This, it will be said, is not Liberalism but Socialism. Pursuing the economic rights of the individual we have been led to contemplate a Socialistic organization of industry. But a word like Socialism has many meanings, and it is possible that there should be a Liberal Socialism, as well as a Socialism that is illiberal. Let us, then, without sticking at a word, seek to follow out the Liberal view of the State in the sphere of economics.

*   *   *

If, then, there be such a thing as a Liberal Socialism—and whether there be is still a subject for inquiry—it must clearly fulfil two conditions. In the first place, it must be democratic. It must come from below, not from above. Or rather, it must emerge from the efforts of society as a whole to secure a fuller measure of justice, and a better organization of mutual aid. It must engage the efforts and respond to the genuine desires not of a handful of superior beings, but of great masses of men. And, secondly, and for that very reason, it must make its account with the human individual. It must give the average man free play in the personal life for which he really cares. It must be founded on liberty, and must make not for the suppression but for the development of personality. How far, it may be asked, are these objects compatible? How far is it possible to organize industry in the interest of the common welfare without either overriding the freedom of individual choice or drying up the springs of initiative and energy? How far is it possible to abolish poverty, or to institute economic equality without arresting industrial progress? We cannot put the question without raising more fundamental issues. What is the real meaning of "equality" in economics? Would it mean, for example, that all should enjoy equal rewards, or that equal efforts should enjoy equal rewards, or that equal attainments should enjoy equal rewards? What is the province of justice in economics? Where does justice end and charity begin? And what, behind all this, is the basis of property? What is its social function and value?

*   *   *

The central point of Liberal economics, then, is the equation of social service and reward. This is the principle that every function of social value requires such remuneration as serves to stimulate and maintain its effective performance; that every one who performs such a function has the right, in the strict ethical sense of that term, to such remuneration and to no more; that the residue of existing wealth should be at the disposal of the community for social purposes. . . . It is, indeed, implied that the State is vested with a certain overlordship over property in general and a supervisory power over industry in general, and this principle of economic sovereignty may be set side by side with that of economic justice as a no less fundamental conception of economic Liberalism. . . .

The distinction that I would claim for economic Liberalism is that it seeks to do justice to the social and individual factors in industry alike, as opposed to an abstract Socialism which emphasizes the one side and an abstract Individualism which leans its whole weight on the other. By keeping to the conception of harmony as our clue we constantly define the rights of the individual in terms of the common good, and think of the common good in terms of the welfare of all the individuals who constitute a society. Thus in economics we avoid the confusion of liberty with competition, and see no virtue in the right of a man to get the better of others. At the same time we are not led to minimize the share of personal initiative, talent, or energy in production, but are free to contend for their claim to adequate recognition. A Socialist who is convinced of the logical coherence and practical applicability of his system may dismiss such endeavours to harmonize divergent claims as a half-hearted and illogical series of compromises. It is equally possible that a Socialist who conceives Socialism as consisting in essence in the co-operative organization of industry by consumers, and is convinced that the full solution of industrial problems lies in that direction, should, in proportion as he considers the psychological factors in production and investigates the means of realizing his ideal, find himself working back along the path to a point where he will meet the men who are grappling with the problems of the day on the principles here suggested, and will find himself able to move forward in practice in the front ranks of economic Liberalism.

*   *   *

The nineteenth century might be called the age of Liberalism, yet its close saw the fortunes of that great movement brought to their lowest ebb. Whether at home or abroad those who represented Liberal ideas had suffered crushing defeats. But this was the least considerable of the causes for anxiety. If Liberals had been defeated, something much worse seemed about to befall Liberalism. Its faith in itself was waxing cold. It seemed to have done its work. It had the air of a creed that is becoming fossilized as an extinct form, a fossil that occupied, moreover, an awkward position between two very active and energetically moving grindstones—the upper grindstone of plutocratic imperialism, and the nether grindstone of social democracy. . . .

Liberalism has passed through its Slough of Despond, and in the give and take of ideas with Socialism has learnt, and taught, more than one lesson. The result is a broader and deeper movement in which the cooler and clearer minds recognize below the differences of party names and in spite of certain real cross-currents a genuine unity of purpose. What are the prospects of this movement? Will it be maintained? Is it the steady stream to which we have compared it, or a wave which must gradually sink into the trough?

To put this question is to ask in effect whether democracy is in substance as well as in form a possible mode of government. To answer this question we must ask what democracy really means, and why it is the necessary basis of the Liberal idea.

*   *   *

The actual future of democracy, however, rests upon deeper issues. It is bound up with the general advance of civilization. The organic character of society is, we have seen, in one sense, an ideal. In another sense it is an actuality. That is to say, nothing of any import affects the social life on one side without setting up reactions all through the tissue. Hence, for example, we cannot maintain great political progress without some corresponding advance on other sides. People are not fully free in their political capacity when they are subject industrially to conditions which take the life and heart out of them. A nation as a whole cannot be in the full sense free while it fears another or gives cause of fear to another. The social problem must be viewed as a whole. We touch here the greatest weakness in modern reform movements. The spirit of specialism has invaded political and social activity, and in greater and greater degree men consecrate their whole energy to a particular cause to the almost cynical disregard of all other considerations. "Not such the help, nor these the defenders" which this moment of the world's progress needs. Rather we want to learn our supreme lesson from the school of Cobden. For them the political problem was one, manifold in its ramifications but undivided in its essence. It was a problem of realizing liberty. We have seen reason to think that their conception of liberty was too thin, and that to appreciate its concrete content we must understand it as resting upon mutual restraint and value it as a basis of mutual aid. For us, therefore, harmony serves better as a unifying conception. It remains for us to carry it through with the same logical cogency, the same practical resourcefulness, the same driving force that inspired the earlier Radicals, that gave fire to Cobden's statistics, and lent compelling power to the eloquence of Bright.

Graham Wallas
LIBERALISM IN AN IRRATIONAL WORLD

Underlying liberal and democratic thinking was the assumption that reason is a universal solvent and that men act in society largely upon rational motives. All the evidence of our times, wrote Graham Wallas (1858–1932), argues against this optimistic illusion. One of the original Fabians, Wallas served on the London County Council and lectured for twenty-eight years at the London School of Economics. He was among the first to grasp the complex spectrum of emotions and habits that motivate men and to emphasize the importance of irrational forces in politics. Two of his most important writings that apply social psychology to political theory are Human Nature in Politics *(1908) and* The Great Society *(1914). The following selection from the first of these reveals how well he grasped the phenomenon of the irrational in society. The reconstruction of liberalism, he believed, rested upon a recognition, rather than a rejection, of irrationality in human behavior.*

The only form of study which a political thinker of one or two hundred years ago would now note as missing is any attempt to deal with politics in its relation to the nature of man. The thinkers of the past, from Plato to Bentham and Mill, had each his own view of human nature, and they made those views the basis of their speculations on government. But no modern treatise on political science, whether dealing with institutions or finance, now begins with anything corresponding to the opening words of Bentham's *Principles of Morals and Legislation*—"Nature has placed mankind under the governance of two sovereign masters, pain and pleasure"; or to the "first general proposition" of Nassau Senior's *Political Economy*—"Every man desires to obtain additional wealth with as little sacrifice as possible." In most cases one cannot ever discover whether the writer is conscious of possessing any conception of human nature at all.

It is easy to understand how this has come about. Political science is just beginning to regain some measure of authority after the acknowledged failure of its confident professions during the first half of the nineteenth century. Bentham's utilitarianism, after supersed-

From Graham Wallas, *Human Nature in Politics* with preface by A. L. Rowse, 4th ed. (Lincoln: University of Nebraska Press, 1962), pp. 35–37, 45–47, 104, 118–119, 203–204, 229–231, 2–3. Reprinted by permission of University of Nebraska Press. Copyright © 1962 by Appleton-Century-Crofts, Inc.

ing both Natural Right and the blind tradition of the lawyers, and serving as the basis of innumerable legal and constitutional reforms throughout Europe, was killed by the unanswerable refusal of the plain man to believe that ideas of pleasure and pain are the only sources of human motive. The "classical" political economy of the universities and the newspapers, the political economy of MacCulloch and Senior and Archbishop Whately, was even more unfortunate in its attempts to deduce a whole industrial polity from a "few simple principles" of human nature. It became identified with the shallow dogmatism by which well-to-do people in the first half of Queen Victoria's reign tried to convince working men that any change in the distribution of the good things of life was "scientifically impossible." Marx and Ruskin and Carlyle were masters of sarcasm, and the process is not yet forgotten by which they slowly compelled even the newspapers to abandon the "laws of political economy," which from 1815 to 1870 stood, like gigantic stuffed policemen, on guard over rent and profits.

When the struggle against *Political Economy* was at its height, Darwin's *Origin of Species* revealed a universe in which the "few simple principles" seemed a little absurd, and nothing has hitherto taken their place. Mr. Herbert Spencer, indeed, attempted to turn a single hasty generalization from the history of biological evolution into a complete social philosophy. He preached what he called "the beneficent working of the survival of the fittest" (*Man versus the State*, p. 50), and Sir Henry Maine called "beneficent private war," a process which they conceived of as no more dangerous than that degree of trade competition which prevailed among English provincial shopkeepers about the year 1884. Mr. Spencer failed to secure even the whole-hearted support of the newspapers; but in so far as his system gained currency it helped further to discredit any attempt to connect political science with the study of human nature.

For the moment, therefore, nearly all students of politics analyse institutions and avoid the analysis of man. The study of human nature by the psychologists has, it is true, advanced enormously since the discovery of human evolution, but it has advanced without affecting or being affected by the study of politics.

*   *   *

Whoever sets himself to base his political thinking on a re-examination of the working of human nature, must begin by trying to overcome his own tendency to exaggerate the intellectuality of mankind.

We are apt to assume that every human action is the result of an intellectual process, by which a man first thinks of some end which he desires, and then calculates the means by which that end can be attained.

. . . If I have a piece of grit in my eye, and ask some one to take it out with the corner of his handkerchief, I generally close the eye as soon as the handkerchief comes near, and always feel a strong impulse to do so. Nobody supposes that I close my eye because, after due consideration, I think it my interest to do so. Nor do most men choose to run away in battle, to fall in love, or to talk about the weather in order to satisfy their desire for a preconceived end. If, indeed, a man were followed through one ordinary day, without his knowing it, by a cinematographic camera and a phonograph, and if all his acts and sayings were reproduced before him next day, he would be astonished to find how few of them were the result of a deliberate search for the means of attaining ends.

*   *   *

The origin of any particular party may be due to a deliberate intellectual process. It may be formed, as Burke said, by "a body of men united for promoting by their joint endeavours the national interest upon some particular principle in which they are all agreed."

But when a party has once come into existence its fortunes depend upon facts of human nature of which deliberate thought is only one. It is primarily a name, which, like other names, calls up when it is heard or seen an "image" that shades imperceptibly into the voluntary realization of its meaning. As in other cases, emotional reactions can be set up by the name and its automatic mental associations. It is the business of the party managers to secure that these automatic associations shall be as clear as possible, shall be shared by as large a number as possible, and shall call up as many and as strong emotions as possible.

*   *   *

The assumption—which is so closely interwoven with our habits of political and economic thought—that men always act on a reasoned opinion as to their interests, may be divided into two separate assumptions: first, that men always act on some kind of inference as to the best means of reaching a preconceived end, and secondly, that all inferences are of the same kind, and are produced by a uniform process of "reasoning."

In such an inquiry one meets the preliminary difficulty that it is very hard to arrive at a clear definition of reasoning. Any one who watches the working of his own mind will find that it is by no means easy to trace these sharp distinctions between various mental states, which seem so obvious when they are set out in little books on psychology. The mind of man is like a harp, all of whose strings throb together; so that emotion, impulse, inference, and the special kind of inference called reasoning, are often simultaneous and intermingled aspects of a single mental experience.

*   *   *

It is true that in America, where politicians have learnt more successfully than elsewhere the art of controlling other men's unconscious impulses from without, there have been of late some noteworthy declarations as to the need of conscious control from within. Some of those especially who have been trained in scientific method at the American Universities are now attempting to extend to politics the scientific conception of intellectual conduct. But it seems to me that much of their preaching misses its mark, because it takes the old form of an opposition between "reason" and "passion." The President of the University of Yale said, for instance, the other day in a powerful address, "Every man who publishes a newspaper which appeals to the emotions rather than to intelligence of its readers . . . attacks our political life at a most vulnerable point." If forty years ago Huxley had in this way merely preached "intelligence" as against "emotions" in the exploration of nature, few would have listened to him. Men will not take up the "intolerable disease of thought" unless their feelings are first stirred, and the strength of the idea of Science has been that it does touch men's feelings, and draws motive power for thought from the passions of reverence, of curiosity, and of limitless hope.

The President of Yale seems to imply that in order to reason men must become passionless. He would have done better to have gone back to that section of the *Republic* where Plato teaches that the supreme purpose of the State realizes itself in men's hearts by a "harmony" which strengthens the motive force of passion, because the separate passions no longer war among themselves, but are concentrated on an end discovered by the intellect.

*   *   *

A hundred years ago a contested election might last in any constituency for three or four weeks of excitement and horseplay, during which the voters were every day further removed from the state of mind in which serious thought on the probable results of their votes was possible. Now no election may last more than one day, and we may soon enact that all the polling for a general election shall take place on the same day. The sporting fever of the weeks during which a general election even now lasts, with the ladder-climbing figures outside the newspaper offices, the flashlights at night, and the cheering or groaning crowds in the party clubs, [is] not only waste of energy but an actual hindrance to effective political reasoning.

A more difficult psychological problem arose in the discussion of the Ballot. Would a voter be more likely to form a thoughtful and public-spirited decision if, after it was formed, he voted publicly or secretly? Most of the followers of Bentham advocated secrecy. Since men acted in accordance with their ideas of pleasure and pain, and since landlords and employers were able, in spite of any laws against intimidation, to bring "sinister" motives to bear upon voters whose votes were known, the advisability of secret voting seemed to follow as a corollary from utilitarianism. John Stuart Mill, however, whose whole philosophical life consisted of a slowly developing revolt of feeling against the utilitarian philosophy to which he gave nominal allegiance till the end, opposed the Ballot on grounds which really involved the abandonment of the whole utilitarian position. If ideas of pleasure and pain be taken as equivalent to those economic motives which can be summed up as the making or losing money, it is not true, said Mill, that even under a system of open voting such ideas are the main causes which induce the ordinary citizen to vote. "Once in a thousand times, as in the case of peace or war, or of taking off taxes, the thought may cross him that he shall save a few pounds or shillings in his year's expenditure if the side he votes for wins." He votes as a matter of fact in accordance with ideas of right or wrong. "His motive, when it is an honourable one, is the desire to do right. We will not term it patriotism or moral principle, in order not to ascribe to the voter's frame of mind a solemnity that does not belong to it." But ideas of right and wrong are strengthened and not weakened by the knowledge that we act under the eyes of our neighbours.

> Since then [wrote John Stuart Mill, April 29, 1865] the real motive which induces a man to vote honestly is for the most part not an interested motive in any form, but a social one, the point to be decided is whether the social feelings connected with an act and the sense of social duty in performing it, can be expected to be as powerful when the act is done in secret, and he can neither be admired for disinterested, nor blamed for mean and selfish conduct. But this question is answered as soon as stated. When in every other act of a man's life which concerns his duty to others, publicity and criticism ordinarily improve his conduct, it cannot be that voting for a member of Parliament is the single case in which he will act better for being sheltered against all comment.

Almost the whole civilized world has now adopted the secret Ballot; so that it would seem that Mill was wrong, and that he was wrong in spite of the fact that, as against the consistent utilitarians, his description of average human motive was right. But Mill, though he soon ceased to be in the original sense of the word a utilitarian, always remained an intellectualist, and he made in the case of the Ballot the old mistake of giving too intellectual and logical an account of political impulses.

*   *   *

[The following extract, from A. L. Rowse's preface to the fourth edition of *Human Nature in Politics* emphasizes the attempt of Wallas to warn liberalism of the danger of holding, "against all the evidence, to a rationalist view of human nature."]

[Liberalism held to] the assumption that human beings largely act in politics upon rational motives and trains of intelligent reasoning. We in our time, alas, know what fatuous nonsense this is. The whole life of the society of our time is strewn with ocular demonstrations of its falsity. Yet this assumption underlies most liberal and democratic thinking on the subject of politics. No wonder Liberalism has been so ineffectual: it consigns itself to futility by clinging to what is so patently untrue of human behavior in the mass. Graham Wallas saw how untrue it was years ago. . . . In short, Liberalism was digging its own grave by sticking blindly, against all the evidence, to a rationalist view of human nature, to what Wallas calls the intellectualist assumption. . . .

Let us get this whole thing in proper perspective. The upshot of it all can be stated quite simply. Wallas was not an irrationalist, any more than I am. What we believe in is the leadership of the irrational forces in society—and, for that matter, in ourselves—by the rational. Of course the opposite way, which was Hitler's, leads to disaster. The proper slogan is—*the leadership of the irrational by the rational.* That means not the superficial rationalism of the nineteenth century, of Bentham and James Mill and the Liberals, which never understood how little rational men are. It needs a deeper, more profound rationalism, which understands men's irrationality, the whole complex of emotions and habit and prejudices that moves them, and can use that understanding for its better guidance and control, to the end of a happier life. There seems to me nothing difficult or original about that; it is in keeping with the whole trend of modern psychology—the field in which the greatest acquisitions to knowledge have been made, I suppose, in our time. Graham Wallas was a pioneer in the application of psychology to political thinking.

A. M. McBriar
LIBERALISM VS. FABIAN SOCIALISM

A. M. McBriar, professor of history at Monash University, Australia, presents the case for the Fabian contribution to liberty and the influence of Fabianism on liberalism. He argues for the dismissal of the charge that Fabians promoted statism and equality at the expense of liberty. Instead, McBriar suggests that the Fabians foresaw one of the major problems of the future and made a distinct contribution to liberty in their interpretation of the function of leisure in an industrial society.

The Fabians stood at the parting of the ways, at the point where the modern attitude to the State diverged from the Liberal-Radical attitude of the nineteenth century. To most modern students, coming to the subject for the first time, the Anarchist view of the State, or the Marxist view that the State will eventually "wither away," seem quite incomprehensible, or at least Utopian optimism of the most extravagant kind. Yet these views were a natural and reasonable development from the Liberal theory which by the nineteenth century had become the predominant view in Western Europe. Beginning in the late seventeenth century, gathering force in the eighteenth, and triumphing in the nineteenth, the Liberal principles had overthrown conservative views which tried to identify State and Society or which allowed the State too large a measure of interference. The Liberals had carefully separated the conception of the State, the coercive agent of society, from the conception of civil society: they saw civil society as a self-acting co-operative mechanism, and they sought to reduce interference of the State to a minimum. The Liberals believed that the State always would retain a minimal role in defence and in the protection of life and property. . . .

The Liberal conception of the State remained plausible so long as the State remained undemocratic (i.e., remained an "organ of class oppression") with the Liberals as an opposition group, or so long as the principles of *laissez faire* were, by and large, regarded as

From A. M. McBriar, *Fabian Socialism and English Politics: 1884–1918* (London: Cambridge University Press, 1962), pp. 73–74, 155–157, 160–162, 258, 348. Reprinted by permission of Cambridge University Press.

desirable. It was, of course, still possible, though difficult, to hold to the Liberal view of the State after the advent of a large measure of democracy, so long as one did not abandon a basically *laissez faire* position—as was demonstrated by John Stuart Mill. But Mill himself was abandoning this position in his later years, and once this had been done, a complete reassessment of the attitude to the State became imperative. Mill's Liberal successors turned for help to the works of Hegel and Comte. Hegel was, perhaps, the better choice. Comte, at a time when theorists were still talking of the diminishing power of the State, had brilliantly predicted that the role of the State of the future would be not less, but greater; but both the practical proposals and the tone of Comte's *Positive Polity* repelled many Liberals.

The restatement of Liberalism by Thomas Hill Green, Bernard Bosanquet, and Edward Caird was a development parallel to, rather than one which promoted, Fabian political thinking. Some leading Fabians, notably Sydney Olivier and Graham Wallas, were at Oxford at the time T. H. Green flourished there, but they do not appear to have come under his influence to any extent. The influence of the Liberal-Hegelians on Fabian thought came rather later, through D. G. Ritchie, who was a member of the Fabian Society from 1889 to 1893, through Sidney Ball, who led the local Fabian Society in Oxford, and through the Webbs' contacts with R. B. Haldane. By then, the Fabians had already set their feet on the new path.

*   *   *

"Mere nationalization, or mere municipalization, of any industry is not Socialism or Collectivism," wrote Sidney Ball, "it may be only the substitution of corporate for private administration; the social idea and purpose with which Collectivism is concerned may be completely absent." What then were the social ideas that were to inspire the changes in "machinery" which the Fabians proposed? At the most general level the dispute between Liberals and Socialists is really a dispute about means rather than ends; the Socialist is as likely as the Liberal to state his ends to be Liberty, Equality, and Fraternity—"the freest and fullest development of human quality and power" that is possible in a community. The Socialist merely claims that the means proposed by *laissez faire* Liberalism are unlikely to achieve these ends, and puts forward alternative means to them. However, it is not only the history of religion which shows that there may be importantly different emphases on the three elements of a trinity. Critics have frequently argued that Socialists in general have emphasized Equality and Fraternity at the expense of Liberty.

It may at least be allowed that equality (at any rate, equality in a special sense) is of the very essence of Socialism. Equality of service, or rather, an equal obligation of all able-bodied members to serve the community by "labour of hand and brain" is a moral duty implicit in Socialists' denunciations of those who "live by owning." This moral claim has lent a powerful driving force to Socialist propaganda: it can be illustrated by almost any of the theoretical Tracts of the Fabian Society, from its very first Tract, which asked indignantly, "What can be said in favour of a system which breeds and tolerates the leisured 'masher,' who lives without a stroke of useful work . . . ?" to the much later one, which in a lighter, but no less deadly vein defined an "independent income" as "an abject and total dependence on the labour of others." Equality of service, in this sense, does not imply that Socialists, Fabian or other, considered that the services contributed to society by individuals would be equal in value, nor that they agreed that individuals should be rewarded equally. Furthermore, the "ideal principle" of Socialism—the rejection of the right to individual proprietorship of the means of production and of the right to receive rent and interest as a consequence of such proprietorship—is, as we have seen earlier, modified quite seriously when it comes to practical application. But, despite these qualifications, Socialism remains basically a claim for the removal of inequalities caused by private ownership of the means of production.

Behind this narrower ideal of equality looms the vaguer and larger vision of the classless society. Some Fabians questioned the possibility of attaining it, and were content to envisage a Socialist society as one in which classes would be based on status or function and not ownership of land or capital. But however cynical Bernard Shaw and other leading Fabians were prepared to be about the "inessentials" of Socialism, this piece of disillusionment did not appeal to them. The disenchanting prospect of a class-divided Socialist society drove Shaw to advocate incomes that were absolutely equal, and to propose the "intermarriageability" test as the criterion for deciding whether a satisfactory degree of equality had been attained. The Webbs' writings, and particularly the denuciations of snobbery and class distinction in Beatrice Webb's Diaries, also leave no doubt that their ideal was some form of classless society. . . .

Fraternity was an ideal much more emphasized by the Independent Labour Party and the Clarion Clubs, and those Fabians who wished to share fully in the comradely spirit became members of these organizations as well. The Fabian Society for its own part remained resolutely middle class and rationalistic.

What, then, of Liberty? Did the Fabians, in their emphasis on Equality, slip unconsciously towards authoritarianism in their ultimate ideals, and fail to keep the delicate balance between Equality and Liberty? Prominent writers have hinted that they did. Halévy suggested they were influenced by the "Prussian model" of social organization and social philosophy. "Well-oiled samurai," remarked O. D. Skelton, "Is this . . . the deceitful harmony of Fascism? The law of the beehive?" asked Sir Alexander Gray of a passage in Sidney Webb's Fabian Essay.

At the outset, it seems necessary to say that there is no difficulty in discovering passages in Fabian literature which show the influence of Hegelian and Platonic philosophy; which imply the acceptance of an "organic" conception of society and fall without doubt into the category of theories which Dr. Popper in his works has labelled "historicism." Again, it is easy to choose from Fabian writing passages which show an almost Comtean emphasis on planning, neatness, efficiency, economy, and hygiene. But how strong must these tendencies be for a school of thought to be labelled totalitarian? And are such ideas always totalitarian or is their historical association with it largely fortuitous?

*   *   *

One could be reluctant to go as far as the Fabians in state regulation; one could even find isolated passages in their works where a rather naive approval seems to be given to regulation in general; but in looking over their work as a whole it would be unjust to accuse them of being unaware that the problem of liberty was involved. Not only was the Fabian Society as a whole, for the greater part of its existence, engaged in urging hardly more than the "national minimum" of planning, much of which nowadays finds approval far outside the ranks of Socialists, but the more subtle theoretical aspects of the "paradox of freedom" were recognized by individual Fabians. "I entirely agree with the old position that a law is an evil which should be avoided where it can be avoided without greater evil," said Webb, in answer to a question before the Royal Commission on Labour, "but of course the case of those who ask for a legal shortening of the hours of labour is that the evil which will result without the law is greater than the evil which the law would cause."

Nor can the Fabians be accused of taking a naive view of Socialism as the "New Jerusalem" where the problem of liberty and all the other problems are automatically solved. "The Fabian Society puts forward Socialism not as a solution of all evils but only of those arising out of the unequal distribution of wealth," declared Tract 70. "Let it be at once admitted," wrote William Clarke,

> that if Collectivism makes every human being a mere function of the whole, a mere pin in the wheel, a mere end to others' purposes, then it is impossible, for every strenuous mind will rise in revolt against it. A mechanical uniform civilization, with complete centralization and tremendous intensity of working power, with the general conditions of life very much as they are now, with the exception that no one could starve, would be a very close approximation to hell, whether closer or not than the present system of society I am not prepared to say.

Webb had the same problem in mind when he insisted on the importance of a careful balance of autonomy and centralization in local government. He hoped to avoid over-centralization by an expansion of local government powers through "Municipal Socialism," and he hoped to preserve variety of structure in organization within the Socialist State.

Liberty Is Leisure

There remains yet another way in which the Fabians sought to increase liberty and which is, indeed, central to their whole Socialist position. Their belief can best be approached from the concept of

"Nature the taskmaster." "Once for all," wrote Shaw, "we are not born free; and we never can be free. When all human tyrants are slain or deposed there will still be the supreme tyrant that can never be slain or deposed, and that tyrant is Nature." The conflict of Man with Nature is used as an explanation of the origin of society (since co-operative effort is a way of doing Nature's tasks with less labour) and of the fact that complete "freedom of restraint" could involve a natural (i.e., economic) oppression more intolerable than a social tyranny. The next part of the argument is summed up in Shaw's short and startling question and answer: "What is liberty? Leisure." It runs as follows: Nature is a taskmaster that requires certain work to be done, and a certain daily routine to be carried out; work, sleep, feeding, resting, etc., are compulsory; when these daily tasks are done, one has *leisure*—a time in which one may do as one pleases (i.e., be at liberty); the function of society and the purpose of new inventions ought to be to increase leisure and enable it to be equitably distributed.

The objection could of course be raised that this does not exhaust the problem of liberty, in either a political or industrial sense, as Shaw's aphorism, and some of the argumentation with which he has supported it, might suggest. Certainly the Guild Socialists did not think so, when they advocated democracy in industry. Nor need one suppose the Fabians, even Shaw himself, really imagined it did. The idea, however, is important in Fabianism, particularly in connection with the Guild Socialist controversy, because it shows that the Fabians thought mainly of increasing liberty *outside* work by shortening working hours. It shows also that they believed that the State should not regulate its citizens' leisure outside their working hours. And, finally, it is important in Shaw's idea of the place of the artist in the Socialist State: he insists that the State can do no good by regulating or pampering its artists, and the only solution is to give them some employment that will leave them plenty of leisure (which will bring them into contact with community life, and yet leave them free to pursue their art). . . .

The Fabians' idea of "freedom outside work" shows at all events that they were not "totalitarian" in the sense of believing that the individual could realize his "true self" only in communal activity. It shows indeed that Liberty as well as Equality was a principal aim of the Fabians, and that they foresaw and courageously tried to deal with a major problem of the future, even if their faith that people would use their leisure for self-improvement is somewhat redolent of an age before the rise of mass amusements.

*   *   *

To what extent was the "New Liberalism" influenced by Fabianism? This is no easy question. It could be maintained that the New Liberalism avoided everything in Fabianism that differed from, or went beyond, late nineteenth century Liberal Progressivism, and in this sense it was not influenced by the Socialism of the Fabians. On the other hand, the "New Liberal" writers had read Fabian works, all of them were in contact with the Fabian leaders, and all were anxious to preserve the Liberal-Labour alliance which seemed threatened by the I.L.P. and the newly-formed Labour Party. Consequently there is a difference in the form, and to a lesser extent in the substance, of "New Liberalism," when compared with the older Progressivism, which enables one to say that it was influenced by Socialist doctrine of the Fabian kind. There was not merely the use of phrases like "national minimum standards," and an acceptance of the ideas embodied in such phrases, but a general recognition also of the increased power and importance of Labour in the State, especially of the Trade Unions, and a recognition likewise of the justice of Labour demands for greater material equality.

*   *   *

So long as Socialists clung to a rigid Marxist dogma they were doomed to remain a tiny and insignificant sect in a country which was still, in the later nineteenth century, the most prosperous country in the world, and which had made half a century of progress since the turbulence of the change to an industrial society. By the time the Fabians appeared English capitalism could afford the luxury of a conscience; and the relatively larger size of the cake to be shared between worker and capitalist, as well as the advent of democracy, made necessary a modification of rigid Marxist formulas. A more accurate claim on behalf of the Fabians would be that the Fabians were the first group in the field with a Socialism suitable for a nation so prosperous, so constitutional, and so respectful of suave and confident authority as England. Only a "Fabian" type of Socialism could have won the allegiance of English trade unionists; that such a Socialism would have made its appearance, even if the Fabians had not supplied it, seems likely; that the Fabians accomplished the theoretical task well seems established by their effective predominance in the field.

England would have been constitutional anyway; the Fabians supplied a doctrine which could enable a churchwarden, or an English trade unionist, to call himself a Socialist. But his conversion, presumably, made a difference to his fundamental assumptions about society and to his ultimate social objectives, for Fabian doctrine, if not original at the highest level, did involve a serious challenge to old-established social opinions. It involved the abandonment of the ideal of a mainly *laissez faire* society and the acceptance of its opposite, the ideal of a society consciously organized; it involved the rejection of the rights of the *rentier,* and the acceptance of a great degree of economic equality; it demanded drastic State action to eliminate poverty. These were, of course, beliefs characteristic of Socialism in general, rather than of Fabianism in particular; but Fabianism permitted Englishmen to swallow these pills without too much shock to their constitution.

IV THE VICTORIAN ADMINISTRATIVE STATE: A REAPPRAISAL

Oliver MacDonagh and Henry Parris
WHICH BENTHAMITE DOCTRINE OF THE STATE?

The liberal accent on freedom in Victorian England found expression in both laissez-faire individualism and state intervention. The one sought to encourage freedom of action; the other, to prevent, through legislative action, the abuse of that freedom. Liberals frequently invoked Bentham's theory of utility to justify either course of action. A. V. Dicey and Elie Halévy based their interpretation of the Victorian state on the laissez-faire doctrine found in Bentham. In turn, J. Bartlett Brebner argued that Bentham was, instead, "the archetype of British collectivism." Each thesis has come under fire in recent years from scholars who are reluctant to attribute so much influence to utilitarianism. Involved also is the larger issue of the role of ideas in shaping men's actions. The opposing arguments in this controversy are provided in the following debate between Oliver MacDonagh, Fellow of St. Catherine's College, Cambridge, and Henry Parris, lecturer in politics at the University of Durham. Each offers a model to explain the nineteenth-century revolution in government. In either case the reader will note that once the social conscience of the nation was pricked by the exposure of an "intolerable" evil, the instinctive moral or humanitarian reaction of Victorians was "to legislate the evil out of existence."

(I)

In very general terms, the change with which we are concerned is the transformation, scarcely glimpsed till it was well secured, of the operations and functions of the state within society, which destroyed belief in the possibility that society did or should consist, essentially or for the most part, of a mere accumulation of contractual relationships between persons, albeit enforced so far as need be by the sovereign power. Now our first proposition is that very powerful impulses towards such a change were generated by a peculiar concatenation of circumstances in the nineteenth century. Again in very general terms, these circumstances were as follows: the unprecedented scale and intensity and the other novelties of

(I) From Oliver MacDonagh, "The Nineteenth-Century Revolution in Government: A Reappraisal," *The Historical Journal,* Vol. I (1958), pp. 57–61, 65–67. Reprinted by permission of Cambridge University Press. (II) From Henry Parris, "The Nineteenth-Century Revolution in Government: A Reappraisal Reappraised," *The Historical Journal,* Vol. III (1960), pp. 28, 33–37. Reprinted by permission of Cambridge University Press.

the social problems arising from steam-powered industrialization, and from the vast increase, and the new concentrations and mobility, of population; the simultaneous generation of potential solutions, or partial solutions, to these problems by the developments in mass production and cheap and rapid transport, by the new possibilities of assembling great bodies of labour, skills and capital, and by the progress of the technical and scientific discovery associated with this economic growth; the widespread and ever-growing influence of humanitarian sentiment and of stricter views of sexual morality and "decency"; the increasing sensitivity of politics to public pressures, and the extraordinary growth in both the volume of legislation and the degree to which its introduction became the responsibility of governments, with the corollaries of changes in parliamentary practice and of the rapid development of parliament's investigatory instruments.

The legislative-cum-administrative process which this concatenation of circumstances set in motion may perhaps best be described by constructing a "model" of its operation. Very simply, the most common origin of this sort of process was the exposure of a social evil. Sometimes, the exposure was sudden and catastrophic, the consequence of an epidemic, a mine explosion, a railway calamity; sometimes, dramatic in another sense, the revelation of a private philanthropist or of an altogether fortuitous observer. On the whole, exposures were, so to speak, exogenous. Rarely were they, in this first instance, the fruit of the practice of administration or regular inquiry. Nor was sensationalism unimportant, for exposures were effective in so far as they directed public or parliamentary attention to particular dangers, suffering, sexual immorality or injustice. Once this was done sufficiently, the ensuing demand for remedy at any price set an irresistible engine of change in motion. Once it was publicized sufficiently that, say, women on their hands and knees dragged trucks of coal through subterranean tunnels, or that emigrants had starved to death at sea, or that children had been mutilated by unfenced machinery, these evils became "intolerable"; and throughout and even before the Victorian years "intolerability" was the master card. No wall of either doctrine or interest could permanently withstand that single trumpet cry, all the more so as governments grew ever more responsive to public sentiment, and public sentiment ever more humane. The demand for remedies was also, in the contemporary context, a demand for prohibitory enactments. Men's instinctive reaction was to legislate the evil out of existence. But at this point the reaction was usually itself resisted. As the threat to legislate took shape, the endangered interests, whatever they might be, brought their political influence into action, and the various forces of inertia, material and immaterial, came into play. Almost invariably, there was compromise. Both in the course of the drafting of the bill, when trade interests often "made representations" or were consulted, and in the committee stage in Parliament, the restrictive clauses of the proposed legislation were relaxed, the penalties for their defiance whittled down and the machinery for their enforcement weakened. None the less the measure, however emasculated, become law. A precedent was established, a responsibility assumed: the first stage of the process was complete.

The second stage began when it was disclosed, sooner or later, gradually or catastrophically, that the prohibitory legislation had left the original evils largely or perhaps even altogether untouched. For, generally speaking, first statutes tended to be ineffective even beyond the concessions yielded to trade and theory in the course of their drafting and passage. This was so because the draftsmen and the politicians (preliminary parliamentary inquiry in some cases notwithstanding) knew little or nothing of the real conditions which they were attempting to regulate, and paid little or no attention to the actual *enforcement* of penalties and achievement of objects. In consequence, the first act was commonly but an amateur expression of good intentions. Of what value was it, for example, to offer remote (and incidentally, irrelevent and insufficient) remedies at common law to very poor and often illiterate men? As James Stephen, with characteristic fatalism, observed of one such case, "These [men] are not the first, nor will they be the last to make the discovery that a man may starve and yet have the best right of action that a special pleader could wish for." Simply, the answer to provide summary processes at law and the like, and special officers to see that they were carried into action; and sooner or later, in one form or other, this was done where mere statute making of the older sort was seen to have been insufficient.

Like the original legislation, the appointment of executive officers was a step of immense, if unforeseen, consequence. Indeed we might almost say that it was this which brought the process into life. There was now for the first time a body of persons, however few, professionally charged with carrying the statute into effect. As a rule, this meant some measure of regulation where before there had been none. It also meant a much fuller and more concrete revelation, through hard experience and manifold failures, of the very grave deficiencies in both the restrictive and executive clauses of the statute; and this quickly led to demands for legislative amendments in a large number of particulars. These demands were made moreover with a new and ultimately irresistible authority. For (once again for the first time) incontrovertible first-hand evidence of the extent and nature of the evils was accumulating in the officers' occasional and regular reports; and there was both a large measure of unanimity in their common-sense recommendations for improvements, and complete unanimity in their insistence upon the urgency of the problems. Finally, side by side with the imperative demand for further legislation, there came an equivalent demand for centralization. This, too, arose as a matter of obvious necessity from the practical day-to-day difficulties of their office. For, without a clearly defined superior authority, the executive officers tended towards exorbitance or timid inactivity or an erratic veering between the two. Usually the original appointment had left their powers and discretions undefined, and usually the original statute was both imprecise and framed before an executive was contemplated. In consequence, the officers' efforts to secure "substantial justice" often led to miserable wrangling, partiality, "despotism" and bad relations with the parties with whose conduct they were concerned. On occasion it even led to counter-prosecution. Thus the officers themselves soon came to recognize the need for an authoritative superior both for the definition of law and status and for protection and support against the anarchic "public." Moreover, centralization was quickly seen to be required for two other purposes, the systematic collection and collation of evidence and proposals for reform and the establishment of an intermediary or link between Parliament and the executive in the field. Sooner or later, the pressures born of experience succeeded in securing both fresh legislation and a superintending central body. The point at which they did may be taken as the culmination of our third phase.

The fourth stage in the process consisted of a change of attitude on the part of the administrators. Gradually it was borne in upon the executive officers, and through them upon the central authority, that even the new amending, and perhaps consolidating, legislation did not provide a fully satisfactory solution. Doubtless, it embodied many or most of their recommendations and effected substantial improvements in the field concerned. But experience soon showed that it was possible, endlessly possible, to devise means of evading some at least of the new requirements, and equally that the practical effects and judicial interpretations of statutory restrictions could not be always or altogether foreseen. Experience also showed, though less rapidly and clearly, that the original concept of the field of regulation—we might almost say the very concept that there were definite boundaries to such a field at all—was much too narrow. Finally, the appetite for regulation (not in the pejorative sense of regulation for regulation's sake but in the sense of a deepening understanding of what might and should be done) tended to grow with every partial success. All this subtly wrought a *volte-face* in the outlook of the administrators. Gradually they ceased to regard their problems as resolvable once for all by some grand piece of legislation or by the multiplication of their own number. Instead, they began to see improvement as a slow, uncertain process of closing loopholes and tightening the screw ring by ring, in the light of continuing experience and experiment. In short, the fourth stage of the process witnessed the substitution of a dynamic for a static concept of administration and the gradual crystallization of an *expertise* or notion of the principles of government of the field in question.

In the fifth and final stage, this new and more or less conscious Fabianism worked itself out into models of government which seem to us peculiarly modern. The executive officers and their superiors now demanded, and to some extent secured, legislation which awarded them discretions not merely in the application of its clauses but even in imposing penalties and framing regulations. They began to undertake more systematic and truly statistical and experimental investigations. They strove to get and to keep in touch with the inventions, new techniques and foreign practices relevant to their field. Later, they even called directly upon medicine and engineering, and the infant professions of research chemistry and biology, to find answers to intractable difficulties in composing and enforcing particular preventive measures; and once, say, ventilation mechanisms or azimuth compasses for ocean-going vessels, or safety devices for mines or railways, or the presence of arsenic in certain foods or drinks, had been clearly proved, the corresponding regulations passed effortlessly into law, and, unperceived, the ripples of government circled ever wider. In the course of these latest pressures towards autonomy and delegated legislation, towards fluidity and experimentation in regulations, towards a division and a specialization of administrative labour, and towards a dynamic role for government within society, a new sort of state was being born. It was modern in a much fuller and truer sense than even Edwin Chadwick's bureaucracy.

Let us repeat that the development outlined above is but a "model," and a "model" moreover which, with a few important exceptions such as slavery reform, applies peculiarly to the half century 1825–1875. It does not necessarily correspond in detail with any specific departmental growth. Even in the fields of social reform where it was most likely to operate "purely," it was not always present. In an exact form, in an unbroken adherence to the pattern, it was perhaps rarely present. Nor are the stages into which the process has been divided to be regarded as sacrosanct or necessarily equal in duration or indeed anything more than the most logical and usual type of development; and it is true, of course, that minor variants and elements have been omitted from the structure for purposes of simplification. To sum up, what has been attempted in the preceding section is simply a description, in convenient general terms, of a very powerful impulse or tendency, always immanent in the middle quarters of the nineteenth century, and extraordinarily often, though by no means invariably, realized in substance.

*   *   *

Benthamism is, of course, a very different matter. In its concern with the regulatory aspects of law and the problems of legal enforcement, in its administrative ingenuity and inventiveness, in its downright rejection of prescription, in its professionalism and its faith in "statistical" inquiry, it worked altogether with the grain of our "revolution." Wherever it was the operative force in these respects, it may be said to have displaced or rendered superfluous the administrative momentum. But we must be very circumspect indeed in deciding that Benthamism was the operative force in any particular instance. Broadly speaking, so far as the administrative matters with which we are concerned go, Benthamism had no influence upon opinion at large or, for that matter, upon the overwhelming majority of public servants. . . . In general, nothing is more mistaken than a "blanket" prima facie assumption that "useful," "rational" or centralizing changes in the nineteenth century were Benthamite in origin.

There are moreover other qualifications to be made upon the Benthamite contribution. In the first place, Benthamism in its later form was heavily entangled with two great anti-collectivist influences, political individualism and the notion of the natural harmony of economic interests; and although a few of those who spoke of themselves as utilitarians preserved Benthamism's hard administrative core through thick and thin, this is by no means true of the majority. . . .

Thus, generally we can say, first, that the genuine contribution of Benthamism to modern government must be measured in terms of particular actions of particular individuals; secondly, that Benthamism, in so far as it took colour from other contemporary ideologies, was an obstacle, after their fashion, to the development of modern government; and thirdly, that "administrative" Benthamism, where it was effective, also made a peculiar, idiosyncratic contribution to nineteenth-century administration, and one which was extraneous and at points antagonistic to the main line of growth.

(II)

If it is wrong to assume that men were influenced by Bentham's ideas, it is equally wrong to assume, as Dr. MacDonagh does, that they were not. . . . In any case, Dr. MacDonagh makes no allowance for the unconscious influence of ideas on men's minds.

*   *   *

Why should anyone seek to eliminate Benthamism as a factor of importance in nineteenth-century history? A possible answer is that it is one way of resolving an apparent contradiction which has puzzled many students of the subject. Some have discerned contradiction within the theory itself. Halévy, for example, contrasted the principle of artificial identification of interests, on which Bentham founded his theory of politics and law, with the principle of natural identity of interests, which appeared fundamental to his view of economics. Sir Cecil Carr has remarked, "How the Benthamites could reconcile [their theory of law] with their natural addiction to the doctrines of *laissez faire* is one of the puzzles of political science." Others have perceived contradictions between theory, on the one hand, and the course of events on the other. Professor Prouty, for example, has written:

> *Laissez faire in early nineteenth century Britain was never a system. . . . While . . . as a general principle or as an argument against a particular measure [it] might continue to receive wide publicity, it was persistently defeated in practice. . . . The most determined liberal could not consistently argue for laissez faire; he sooner or later found himself advocating a measure which involved the Government in the regulation of some part of industry. State intervention may not have been the policy but it was the growing reality.*

Dr. MacDonagh is similarly puzzled; he begins one of his valuable papers by saying that it "is concerned with the extraordinary contrast between this appearance of a 'free society' and the realities of the situation"; and ends, "We have seen how a 'despotic' form of administrative discretion came into being almost casually in the very hey-day of liberal individualism and *laissez-faire*."

An extreme solution to this problem was propounded by the late Professor Brebner. His attitude to Dicey resembles that of Marx towards Hegel. Dissatisfied with his argument, he sought to correct it by turning it the other way up. Dicey had assumed that the consequences of Benthamism were limited, in practice, to the promotion of *laissez-faire*. Brebner suggests, on the other hand, that "Laissez faire was a political and economic myth in the sense formulated by Georges Sorel." But "although laissez faire never prevailed in Great Britain or in any other modern state, many men today have been led to believe that it did. In this matter . . . Dicey . . . seems to have been the principal maintainer of the myth for others." *Law and Opinion* "amounted to an argument against increasing collectivism. The lectures were so passionately motivated as to be a sincere, despairing, and warped reassertion of the myth in terms of legal and constitutional history . . . . In using Bentham as the archetype of British individualism he was conveying the exact opposite of the truth. Jeremy Bentham was the archetype of British collectivism." Developments of *laissez-faire* did of course take place; but these Brebner attributes to a separate current of opinion, deriving ulti- mately from Adam Smith, and though often working in alliance with Benthamism, never assimilated to it.

Valuable as a corrective to Dicey, Brebner's argument is too violent a reaction against it. The twin themes of his paper—*laissez- faire* and state intervention—were equally characteristic develop- ments of the middle quarters of the nineteenth century, and it is not necessary to assume that they were in contradiction to one another. Professor Robbins has shown how they were reconciled in the field of economic theory. He denies Halévy's argument that there was a contradiction between the assumptions underlying Bentham's theory of law, on the one hand, and classical economics, on the other. The latter was not based on an assumed identity of interests. "If the classical economists assumed anywhere a harmony, it was never a harmony arising in a vacuum but always very definitely within a framework of law. . . . they regarded the appropriate legal frame- work and the system of economic freedom as two aspects of one and the same social process." They advocated free enterprise as the general rule in economic affairs on the grounds that it was the system most likely to benefit the consumer. But they recognized no natural right of free enterprise. Like any other claim to freedom, it had to be justified by the principle of utility. As a rule, it was so justified; but there were many situations (e.g., where producers enjoyed a monopoly) where the State should intervene.

Following this lead, it is possible to suggest a model which avoids the difficulties inherent in those discussed above, while taking into account all the facts enumerated. Its stages are as follows:

1.   The nineteenth-century revolution in government, though a

response to social and economic change, cannot be understood without allowing for the part played in it by contemporary thought about political and social organization; to adopt Dicey's terminology, there was a close connexion between law and opinion.

2. In the relationship between law and opinion, the nineteenth century falls into two periods only, with the dividing line about 1830.

3. Throughout the second of these periods, the dominant current of opinion was Utilitarianism.

4. The main principle of Utilitarianism was what its supporters themselves believed and asserted—the principle of utility. The application of this principle led to considerable extensions both of *laissez-faire* and of State intervention simultaneously.

5. Once special officers had been appointed to administer the law, they themselves played a leading role in legislation, including the development of their own powers.

. . . The first stage (as also the last) incorporates factors which Dicey ignored, and to which Dr. MacDonagh rightly calls attention. But there is nothing inevitable about the process by which institutions respond to changes in the society around them. The nineteenth-century revolution in government was one example of such a response; the French Revolution, and the Hitler regime, were others. One essential factor differentiating the three situations is the nature and quality of current thought about society, its problems, and their solution. It would be absurd to argue that Bentham revolutionized the British system of government by power of abstract thought alone. His ideas were influential because they derived from the processes of change going on around him. He was working with the grain. But it does not follow that the same solutions would have been reached had he never lived.

The second point does not deny that there was a change in the tone of legislation after about 1870. But it resulted from such factors as the Great Depression, the extension of the franchise, and pressure from the administration itself, rather than from the adoption of a hypothetical philosophy of collectivism. Utilitarianism was at work throughout—"that current of thought which arises in Bentham at the beginning of the century and flows into Fabianism at its end."

The fourth point may appear something of a paradox. Yet at the time, there were those who believed in both principles simultaneously. Nassau Senior, for example, believed in *laissez-faire*, but not in the "nightwatch-man" conception of the State. . . . So celebrated an advocate of State intervention as Chadwick still allocated a large, though limited, area to private enterprise:

> *He had great faith in self-interest. He commended it as the spring of individual vigour and efficiency; and it figures prominently in his thought as the most persistent and calculable element in human character. But he saw no evidence at all that social benefits resulted of necessity from its pursuit, and much which persuaded him that without the barriers erected by the law its undirected energies might disrupt society. He put his trust, therefore, not in the rule of some "invisible hand" blending the interests of the individual and society in a mystic reconciliation, but in the secular authority of the State which, abandoning the superstitions of* laissez-faire, *should intervene to guide the activities of individuals towards the desirable goals of communal welfare.*

When, therefore, existing institutions were subjected to the test of utility the result might be either more free enterprise or less. When it was asked "Do the Corn Laws tend to the greatest happiness of the greatest number?" the answer (in 1846) was "No." When it was asked "Since free competition does not work in the field of railway enterprise, would public regulation tend to the greatest happiness of the greatest number?" the answer (in 1840) was "Yes." The question was then, as indeed it is today, not *laissez-faire or* State intervention, but where, in the light of constantly changing circumstances, the line between them should be drawn.

Dr. MacDonagh has done well to draw the attention of administrative historians to the importance of factors which Dicey did not take into account. Some of these were external, such as economic and technical change; others were internal, for example, the influence of the administrators on legislation. Few would deny the importance of these factors, although little has been done so far to work out their implications in detail. In this respect, his studies of the regulation of emigrant traffic are important pioneer work. He has shown that it is possible to account for the development of one minor branch of central administration without considering the influence of Benthamism. But he has not shown that other branches developed in a similar way, as would be necessary to sustain his thesis that Benthamism was a factor of, at most, very minor importance. The accepted view holds the field; namely, that the nineteenth-century revolution in government, though not attributable to Benthamism as sole cause, cannot be understood without allotting a major part to the operation of that doctrine.

G. Kitson Clark
THE ADMINISTRATOR AND THE STATE

In this concluding selection G. Kitson Clark, Fellow of Trinity College, Cambridge, and University Reader in Constitutional History from 1954–1967, argues for the centrality of liberty to liberalism. Whether or not the liberal state can withstand the pressures of twentieth-century collectivism, Clark claims that, given the political and social circumstances of nineteenth-century Britain, an "elaborate social policy" and "an increasingly powerful secular state" were more or less inevitable. Since most legislation made the state the instrument for implementing change, it was the administrator on the spot who played the pivotal role, rather than any particular political philosophy or program, in fashioning the collectivist shape of the modern state. Clark's gracefully written essay may make it necessary for the reader to resist the charm of the style in order to examine critically the thesis which he presents. Among Clark's other writings are The Making of Victorian England *(1962) and* Peel and the Conservative Party *(1964).*

A philosophy of liberty . . . . could never be a wholly adequate philosophy because, if you have any social values, freedom is never a sufficient answer to all problems. Apart from the expanding needs of government in any form of society there would always be helpless people on the hands of the public . . . , who could not be trusted

From G. Kitson Clark, *An Expanding Society, Britain 1830–1900* (Cambridge: Cambridge University Press, 1967), pp. 13–14, 48–49, 51, 53, 130, 137–139, 146–147, 163, 180–182. Reprinted by permission of Melbourne University Press.

to look after themselves, and for whom therefore not freedom but active protection and control was needed. As a result, it was quite impossible to have a completely *laissez faire* state. Recent history had emphasized this fact. There had been in the sixteenth and seventeenth centuries a heavily regulated state in England, with wages, the price of beer, of bread, and terms of employment all carefully controlled. People had ceased to believe in the value of such controls and in the eighteenth and nineteenth centuries these things had either fallen quietly into desuetude or the legislation which enforced them had been repealed. But it proved to be impossible to maintain a vacuum in this matter. A state which does nothing for anybody and lets everyone go his own way is virtually impossible. Before the last of the old legislation had been repealed, the first of the factory laws to protect children had come into existence, while there was no real break, from the Middle Ages onwards right up to the great Charter of 1854, in the laws dealing with seamen. These things could, however, all be dismissed as exceptions to the prevailing philosophy, the more easily as in most cases people did not realize how many exceptions were being permitted, or what they were portending. It was only after 1870 that collectivism began to close in on freedom and to such an extent that a new conception of liberalism became necssary, if liberalism it could still be called.

*   *   *

It is clear that in using the phrase—"the fate of Liberalism"—I might be referring to several different things. . . . It might mean, and in the minds of many people it would naturally mean, the fate of that social and economic conception which supported the belief that the best social values could be assured by liberating them from unnecessary interference by the State or by anyone else. Thus, many people believed that trade should be freed to find its most profitable routes; that taxation should be kept down to a minimum, particularly indirect taxation, because that pressed upon the poor; that people should be encouraged to do things for themselves, partly because that encouraged self-reliance, partly because they were the best judges of what they wanted, and partly also because they had an inherent right to decide things for themselves. And to this view of Liberalism, as to all views of Liberalism, should be attached these important basic principles, relating to the freedom of the individual, which had been worked out in the long story of English history: the rule of law and the protection of the individual against arbitrary treatment by the State, equality before the law, freedom of opinion, freedom of worship, and so on.

Much of that Liberal creed is out of fashion nowadays, indeed much of it could not be sustained throughout the nineteenth century. Many essential services could not be supplied by voluntary effort. It was necessary to have public elementary education, although old-fashioned Nonconformists objected to it; indeed, it was necessary to make all children go to school. It was necessary to impose on all cities and towns a minimum standard of cleanliness and hygiene. It was necessary to pass Acts to control the operation of the rail-ways. It was necessary to pass Acts to protect children and even adults in factories. It was necessary to pass Acts to prevent the pollution of food, of rivers, and of the atmosphere. Each particular interference became cumulative, increasingly formidable and exten-sive, and new areas of state interference were constantly developing so that by the end of the century the age of collectivism had un-avoidably succeeded the age of *laissez faire.*

*   *   *

Therefore, if by Liberalism is meant the social and economic policy of Mr Gladstone, it really went out with the nineteenth cen-tury. Possibly the last of the Liberals was that luscious autumn blos-som, Sir William Vernon Harcourt; though some connoisseurs might name Campbell-Bannerman and John Morley.

However, the fate of Liberalism can mean something more serious than this. Liberalism was a peace-loving creed. It depended ex-plicitly on free discussion, the appeal to reason, free elections, the constitutional process, and abstinence from force. But from early in the twentieth century men showed a tendency to turn from these things to violence. Ulster armed to fight Home Rule and the Irish nationalists to fight Ulster. The suffragettes used violent means to draw attention to their cause. Between 1909 and 1913 there was probably more continuous and widespread industrial warfare than ever before; this was not perhaps an actual appeal to violence, but it was not an appeal to reason either.

*　　　*　　　*

Since 1914, and still more since 1933, the world has had its bellyful of violence, and . . . men and women have lost their sense of the value of that element which . . . does seem to be essential to Liberalism, the belief in the value of liberty.

Perhaps that belief starts to go as collectivism necessarily takes the place of *laissez faire.* A reasonable answer to any claim on behalf of personal liberty has been to say—"What is the value of liberty when a man is ill-educated, unhealthy, and intolerably housed?" Theoretically it should be possible to renew that claim for liberty when those physical disabilities have been removed or reduced; practically such a renewal is normally useless for by that time men have learnt to obey, and the State has acquired powers which it is unwilling to surrender. Nor is it clear that the beliefs which many people entertain nowadays will either make people desire that men and women should make free choices for themselves, or sustain a claim that they have a right to do so. For if, as many believe, men and women are only complicated mechanisms set in motion by reflex actions it is difficult to see what the phrase "to make a free choice" can possibly mean, and if the basis of philosophy is frankly materialistic, as it is for many people, then it is difficult to see that the word "right" can imply more than convenience based on that potentially tyrannical doctrine, the greatest happiness of the greatest number. Therefore neither modern habit, nor yet modern principle, would sem to support that belief in human liberty which was deemed to be essential to the creed of Liberalism in the past.

*　　　*　　　*

From 1830 onwards a formidable governmental machine was being created in Britain which brought much of the conduct of life and the use of property under the control of the State, and provided precedents for more extensive controls when the time of need came. It came into existence before the necessities of the twentieth century had revealed themselves. It is sometimes believed that it came into existence as an answer to the exigent demands of a democratized electorate, but in fact it had begun effectively to develop before, in some cases long before, the Reform Act of 1867 and during the period of aristocratic preponderance. It also came into existence while the old ideas of the importance of freedom and self-help still predominated in the minds of most men. Why, then, did this happen? And how did it happen?

I believe the answer to the first question lies very largely not in the realm of theory but in that of fact. From 1830 onwards, indeed from before 1830, Britain had to suffer the results of the industrial revolution and the population explosion. She confronted the conditions which developed with a conscience made sensitive by the workings of the humanitarian movement and the religious revival which had begun in the eighteenth century. This meant she had to undertake a number of tasks which only the public power could tackle. Towns of a size never known in the country before had to be cleansed and policed and supplied with water. The public behaviour of industry had to be disciplined in the interests of those who were its neighbours, the hours of women and children in mill and mine had to be limited, and the conditions under which even adult men laboured had to be controlled. At some time the myriads of children who had come swarming into the world would have to be educated. If these tasks were neglected not only would oppression and misery result but disease and social danger would inevitably follow in their train.

*   *   *

If, however, the initiative in social policy did not necessarily lie with the government there might be circumstances which could force the development of it into government hands, and these might even secure that part of any further initiative passed to men in the government service. There is an early example of this in the history of factory legislation. When in 1833 Lord Ashley, who had become the sponsor for factory reform, proposed the Ten Hours Bill, he met with such stubborn opposition that in the end in despair he yielded up the question to the Whig government. They, in order to settle the matter, promptly passed a measure of their own. This gave much less than the factory reformers desired, but it was a contrast to previous factory Acts in the fact that, whereas they had been inoperative, the Bill of 1833 contained a provision to make sure it came into force, for it was to be operated by four inspectors who were to have the powers of magistrates.

These inspectors would necessarily be the servants of the central government. They would be paid by the government, they would report to the government, and in due course a minister of the Crown would have to be responsible for them. Their appointment was a recognition of the fact that if a social policy was to be effective government machinery would have to be created to put it into force, since it was no good trusting either to self-help or to the ordinary operations of the law, even when it had been reinforced by specially directed statutes. From this fact springs the development of a great deal of the machinery of the modern State. As a matter of fact these inspectors were not quite the first examples of this development, but it is convenient to start with them. They are an obvious precedent for much that was to come and they are also an example of another factor which was to be of considerable importance. They were instructed to meet together to concert regulations and to report. Thus was created an expert official opinion on which future administration would be based and which all future legislation must take into account; indeed many of the clauses of the next factory Act, that of 1844, were based on their recommendations.

This suggests an important possibility. Not only was the State equipping itself with officials with direct executive authority to put its commands into effect, but it was also gaining an intelligence service which would enable it to accumulate expert and professional knowledge based on experiment and experience on the subjects of social policy. This would certainly lead to future legislation based on an understanding of the deficiencies of past laws, and, more than that, the administrators themselves would become the most expert guides for the social policy of the future.

The full possibilities of this suggestion can be realized not so much by looking at the factory inspectors as at the man who invented them. When the government desired to produce a Bill on the factory question as an alternative to Ashley's they instructed Edwin Chadwick to draw it up. For Chadwick had served as one of the commissioners in an enquiry into the factory question, which had been set up as a counter to the report of the select committee which

Sadler [a Tory radical who headed a Parliamentary committee investigating child labor in cotton mills in 1832] had dominated. It was Chadwick who originated the idea of inspectors to enforce the Act, and he was soon to be the author of much more important legislative and administrative developments. He had been seconded to the enquiry into the factory question from his work as one of the commissioners enquiring into the operation of the Poor Laws and the new Poor Law of 1834 was largely based upon his ideas.

*   *   *

Chadwick's relative independence, the fact that he was able to appeal directly to public opinion, enabled the movement for public health to get started. It is difficult to see how otherwise this could have happened. If Chadwick had been enclosed in a fully organized government department speaking only through the mouth of a responsible minister, unable to use the expedients he did use to gain public support, it seems unlikely that in those days he would have accomplished very much. It was the lag in the development of the institutions of Parliamentary government that enabled the knowledge of the expert to be used for the development of social policy as it was used in the two middle quarters of the nineteenth century. When that lag came to an end there was a change and a retardation.

It was this development of social policy that led to the creation of the State as we know it nowadays in Britain. It was not the work of governments pursuing coherent policies, still less was it the legacy of any particular party or the result of the general adoption of any particular philosophy. It was the work of individuals reacting as best they might to particular problems and situations, individual ministers, individual members of Parliament, individual civil servants, and individual members of the general public. Since this was so the work was piecemeal and sporadic, and for this reason not only did contemporaries not understand the significance of what was happening, but even historians writing in later times have not always realized how much was done before 1867 and to what extent what was done after 1870 was a consolidation, if also an extension, of what had been initiated earlier in the century.

*   *   *

I would suggest that what happened between 1830 and 1870, or between 1820 and 1880 for that matter, is, clearly, the immediate result of the reactions of a large number of different people, some of whom I have mentioned by name, many of whom I have not, to the problems which the circumstances of their day presented to them. What they thought about these circumstances was no doubt conditioned by their principles, Tory or Radical, Economist, or Benthamite, Christian or Medical, and by their professional training or experience, and by their temperaments, sensitive, missionary, or negative. What they thought affected what they did, but a preponderant factor in any decision they had to make was always the need to find a practical solution to the immediate problem which necessity, or their sense of humanity, presented to them; and that need might easily override preconceived principles.

*　　*　　*

By 1908 the constitutional changes of the nineteenth century had been completed. The doctrine of ministerial responsibility covered effectively all the executive actions of government servants, and the personal activities of the permanent civil service were restrained by known rules. . . . On the whole the theory of democracy was accepted and with it the doctrine of mandate. And if that doctrine was, as it is always, rather illusory, there was, at least after 1906, a more conscious intention to direct and expand social policy on the part of government.

Behind this new constitutional and political position there was a wider acceptance of the need and propriety of interference by the State in the social life of the country. Not only were there important organized groups openly working for that end, such as the Labour party or the Fabian Socialists, but there were many more who consciously accepted some form of collectivism as a necessary instrument for social decency and justice, and more still who were advocating policies, or themselves developing services, which must end in the extension of state action. For it is one of the most striking lessons of the twentieth century that the State is the residuary legatee of most of the generous enthusiasms and endeavours of public-spirited men and women. . . .

If, however, the mid-Victorian period is considered by itself, the lesson which it seems to teach most eloquently is the great influence in human affairs of the force of necessity, of the pressure of circumstances. Most intelligent and influential people in Victorian England believed to a greater or less extent in self-help, the avoidance of state control, government economy, and the anxious preservation of human freedom. Yet they started to build one of the most effective systems of state government in Europe, and they had to do so. Certainly what they did was at every point directed by human intelligence and moulded by human ideas. Many different people were involved in this work and their thought and their characters made a difference to what was done. If they had been different, or their opportunities and fortunes had been different, or if other people had taken their places, what would have been done would have been different. Some of it might have been better, some worse. Some of it would have come more slowly, some more quickly. All of it might have had a different design. But it seems impossible to doubt that given the circumstances of Britain in the nineteenth century something resembling what did happen would have happened, whoever the agents available might have been.

For at the end I return to what I said at the beginning. Here was a community trying to live in an overcrowded island with a constantly growing population. It was faced by the problems of ever-increasing urbanization. It had to respond to the challenges and opportunities of the industrial and scientific revolutions. It was increasingly enlightened and disturbed by the leaven of humanitarian and religous feeling which had begun to work in it in the eighteenth century, and it was subject to the slowly mounting demands of democracy. Such circumstances made an increasingly elaborate social policy necessary. Such a policy could only be put into effect by an increasingly powerful secular state. Some men may have seen the general direction in which they were travelling, others certainly did not. It did not matter. It is to be doubted whether what was coming into existence was exactly what anyone's principles or prejudices had led him to desire or to expect, since eighteenth-century optimism, the principle of the ultimate natural identity of human interests, is as implicit in much of Benthamism as it is in Communism. But men's intentions had to conform, not to what was recommended by theory, but to what was demanded by fact, and they were not masters of the future.

Suggestions for Additional Reading

English liberalism is primarily a nineteenth-century phenomenon, although it is by no means confined to that century alone. Unfortunately, the nineteenth century is without a bibliographer to provide a comprehensive guide to its historical literature such as Conyers Read, Godfrey Davis, and Stanley Pargellis provide for the three earlier centuries of English history. The interested student would do well to orient himself by consulting a few standard histories as an introduction to the period. Perhaps the most useful for the critical time span of our topic is Robert Ensor's volume in the distinguished Oxford Series, *England, 1870–1914* (London, 1936), but its annotated bibliography is now out of date. For a recent general bibliography of these years, see J. Clive, "British History, 1870–1914, Reconsidered," *American Historical Review,* Vol. LXVIII (1963). The volume preceding Ensor's in the Oxford Series is *The Age of Reform, 1815–1870,* 2nd ed. (London, 1962), by E. L. Woodward. Both volumes offer a valuable assessment of the whole spectrum of English society.

Elie Halévy's six-volume *History of the English People in the Nineteenth Century,* 2nd ed. (New York, 1949–1952), although weak in its coverage of the middle years, is still indispensable for its keen analysis, now under attack, of the forces involved in the dialectic between laissez faire and collectivism. Three of the best brief histories of the period are Asa Briggs, *The Age of Improvement, 1783–1867* (London, 1964), David Thomson, *England in the Nineteenth Century,* Pelican Series (London, 1950), and G. M. Trevelyan, *British History in the Nineteenth Century and After,* 2nd ed. (London, 1937). The best single work on mid-Victorian England—and a delight to read—is G. M. Young's *Victorian England: Portrait of an Age,* 2nd ed. (New York, 1964). Narrower in time span but inclusive in subject matter is *Edwardian England, 1901–1914* (New York, 1964), a collection of essays edited by Simon Nowell-Smith. This highly selective list of general works concludes with G. Kitson Clark's perceptive observations on ideas and men in his Ford lectures delivered at Oxford University, *The Making of Victorian England* (Cambridge, Mass., 1962).

No comparable work to Leslie Stephen's *History of English Thought in the Eighteenth Century,* 2 volumes, 2nd ed. (London, 1881), exists for the Victorian period. Three very readable surveys, however, are Crane Brinton, *English Political Thought in the Nine-teenth Century,* 2nd ed. (Cambridge, Mass., 1949), George H. Sabine, *A History of Political Theory,* 3rd ed. (London, 1963), Chapters XXX–XXXII, and Sir Ernest Barker, *Political Thought in England, 1848–1914,* 2nd ed. (London, 1928). The last volume, in the Home University Library series, is remarkably lucid. D. C. Somervell attempts to study thought in the form of opinion, instead of philosophy, in *English Thought in the Nineteenth Century,* 5th ed. (New York, 1947). F. J. C. Hearnshaw edits two volumes of rather uneven short essays on literary and political writers: *The Social and Political Ideas of Some Representative Thinkers of the Age of Reaction and Reconstruction, 1815–1865* (New York, 1932) and *The Social and Political Ideas of Some Representative Thinkers of the Victorian Age* (New York, 1933). Basil Willey contributes a helpful volume, *Nine-teenth Century Studies: Coleridge to Matthew Arnold* (New York, 1949), in his valuable series on the intellectual and literary back-grounds of recent centuries. A first-rate account of Victorian person-alities and the intellectual excitement and paradoxes they provide is *Victorian Minds* (New York, 1968) by Gertrude Himmelfarb. Other interpretations of the nineteenth-century intellectual and literary mi-lieu are Jerome H. Buckley, *The Victorian Temper: A Study in Lit-erary Culture* (Cambridge, Mass., 1969) and Walter Houghton, *The Victorian Frame of Mind, 1830–1870* (New Haven, 1957).

A full-scale history of English liberalism has yet to be written. W. L. Blease traces the course of liberalism in English politics from 1760 to 1910 in *A Short History of English Liberalism* (New York, 1913), but the volume suffers from partisanship and obsolescence. William A. Orton attempts to update the account in *The Liberal Tra-dition* (New Haven, 1945). A brief, but brilliant, exposition of liberal-ism is found in the introduction to *The Liberal Tradition: From Fox to Keynes* (London, 1956), a book of readings edited by Alan Bullock and Maurice Shock. More plentiful are specialized studies within the broad framework of English liberalism. For the "classical" or laissez-faire phase of liberalism three analyses of the "dismal sci-ence" are helpful: Mark Blaug, *Ricardian Economics: A Historical Study* (New Haven, 1958), Lionel Robbins, *The Theory of Economic Policy in English Classical Political Economy* (London, 1952), and W. D. Grampp, *The Manchester School of Economics* (Oxford, 1960). The cluster of ideas identified with "individualism" and with English political and economic liberalism is discussed in K. W. Swart's "Individualism in the Mid-Nineteenth Century," *Journal of the History of Ideas,* Vol. XXIII (1962). Gladstone's commitment to the principle of liberty and the peculiarities in his mode of applying the principle are carefully documented in "Gladstone on Liberty and Democracy," *Review of Politics,* Vol. XXIII (1961), by David Nicholls. The philosophical radicals, along with the classical economists, provided the twin drive shafts for early liberalism. The classic studies on the ideas of the Benthamite radicals are Elie Halévy's *Growth of Philosophical Radicalism* (London, 1928) and Leslie Stephen's, *The English Utilitarians,* 3 volumes (New York, 1900). See also John P. Plamenatz, *The English Utilitarians,* 2nd ed., rev. (Oxford, 1958). A recent study incorporating Bentham's arguments is Shirley Letwin's *The Pursuit of Certainty: David Hume, Jeremy Bentham, John Stuart Mill, Beatrice Webb* (Cambridge, 1965).

On the conflict between individualism and collectivism that characterizes liberalism in flux, see Bernard Bosanquet, *The Philosophical Theory of the State* (London, 1899), W. S. Jevons, *The State in Relation to Labour,* 4th ed. (New York, 1968), and Helen Lynd, *England in the Eighteen-eighties: Toward a Social Basis for Freedom* (New York, 1945). Henry Pelling provides a highly readable account of this era in his *Popular Politics and Society in Late Victorian Britain* (London, 1968). Somewhat analagous in point of view to Spencer's position on laissez-faire individualism is *A Plea for Liberty* (London, 1891), a volume of essays edited by T. Mackay. The popular application of biology to politics, seen in the works of Spencer, Hobson, and Hobhouse, is also found in T. H. Huxley, *Evolution and Ethics* (London, 1893).

Nonconformity identified readily with liberalism and the Liberal party. The best account for the first half of the nineteenth century is R. G. Cowherd's *The Politics of English Dissent: The Religious Aspects of Liberal and Humanitarian Reform Movements from 1815 to 1848* (London, 1959). Except for John F. Glaser's "English Nonconformity and the Decline of Liberalism," *American Historical Review,* Vol. LXIII (1958), there is no detailed study on the interlocking fortunes of Nonconformity and political liberalism. The relationship is discussed, along with other topics, in F. H. Herrick, "Origins of the National Liberal Federation," *Journal of Modern History,* Vol. XVII (1945), Eric Routley, *English Religious Dissent* (Cambridge,

1960), John W. Grant's *Free Churchmanship in England, 1870–1940* (London, 1955), and John Kent, "Hugh Price Hughes and the Nonconformist Conscience," *Essays in Modern Church History in Memory of Norman Sykes* (London, 1966), edited by G. V. Bennett and J. D. Walsh.

Irish Home Rule served as the catalyst for clarifying the ideological basis of English liberalism, according to Lawrence J. McCaffrey's *The Irish Question, 1800–1922* (Lexington, Ky., 1968). The best account of the Irish issue is found in John L. Hammond, *Gladstone and the Irish Nation* (London, 1964). The "New Liberalism" that dominated the turn of the century is espoused, along with Hobson's and Samuel's programs, in Winston Churchill, *Liberalism and the Social Problem,* 3rd ed. (London, 1969). A more detailed examination of the social legislation introduced by the Liberals before World War I intervened is found in Bentley B. Gilbert's *The Evolution of National Insurance in Great Britain: The Origins of the Welfare State* (London, 1966) and in Samuel J. Hurwitz's "The Development of the Social Welfare State in Prewar Britain, 1906–1914," *The Making of English History* (New York, 1952), edited by Robert Schuyler and Herman Ausubel. Two studies that dramatize the dilemma of adapting liberalism to a mass urban democracy are C. F. G. Masterman's *The Condition of England* (London, 1911), written with religious feeling, and George Dangerfield's provocative interpretation of the new patterns of violence emerging in England (1910–1914) in *The Strange Death of Liberal England* (London, 1936).

English liberalism is also illuminated by comparison with liberalism in a larger geographical and historical context. An excellent introductory essay is "European Liberalism in the Nineteenth Century," *American Historical Review,* Vol. LX (1955), by David Harris. The student will also find helpful Guido de Ruggiero, *A History of European Liberalism,* translated into English by R. G. Collingwood (Oxford, 1927), and Frederick M. Watkins, *The Political Tradition of the West: A Study in the Development of Modern Liberalism* (Cambridge, Mass., 1948). Also of value are John H. Hallowell, *The Decline of Liberalism as an Ideology with Particular Reference to German Politico-legal Thought* (Berkeley, 1943), Herbert Marcuse, *Reason and Revolution: Hegel and the Rise of Social Theory,* 2nd ed. (New York, 1954), Theodore Schieder, "The Crisis of Bourgeois Liberalism," *The State and Society in our Times* (London, 1962), Max

Savelle, *Is Liberalism Dead? And Other Essays* (Seattle, 1967), and John Maynard Keynes, *The End of Laissez Faire* (London, 1926). Anglo-American utilitarianism is the focus of P. A. Palmer, "Benthamism in England and America," *American Political Science Review,* Vol. XXXV (1941). An interesting interpretation of American liberalism which indicts pluralism (special interests) and prescribes a return to idealism is *The End of Liberalism* (New York, 1969), by Theodore J. Lowi.

The most valuable readings for the study of English liberalism are, of course, the writings of its political theorists and practitioners (or antagonists), as examined in this book. In addition to the sources of each selection in this volume, the following works are essential for an expansion of their views on liberalism and the state: John Ramsey McCulloch (ed.), *The Works of David Ricardo* (London, 1852); John Stuart Mill, *On Liberty and Considerations on Representative Government* (Oxford, 1948), edited by R. B. McCallum; Mill, *Autobiography* (New York, 1924); Matthew, Arnold, "The Future of Liberalism," *Nineteenth Century,* Vol. XLI (1888); and Herbert Spencer, *Social Statics* (London, 1850) and *The Man Versus the State* (London, 1884). T. H. Green's political thought is almost wholly contained in *The Principles of Political Obligation,* printed in volume two of the *Works of Thomas Hill Green,* 3 volumes (London, 1894–1900), edited by R. L. Nettleship. Other works by contributors to this volume are D. G. Ritchie, *Darwinism and Politics* (London, 1889), Leonard T. Hobhouse, *The Metaphysical Theory of the State* (London, 1918), and John A. Hobson, *Problems of Poverty,* 4th ed. (London, 1968).

Equally illuminating is biographical history in noting the transformations in English liberalism. Five biographies are particularly valuable: Philip Magnus, *Gladstone: A Biography* (New York, 1964), Michael Packe, *The Life of John Stuart Mill* (London, 1954), D. A. Hamer, *John Morley: Liberal Intellectual in Politics* (London, 1968); the *Life of Joseph Chamberlain,* 4 volumes (London, 1932–1951), by J. L. Garvin and Julian Amery, is a rich mine of political information, while Melvin Richter provides a keen analysis of Green and his political theories in *The Politics of Conscience: T. H. Green and his Age* (London, 1964). The reader is also directed to John Morley's *Life of Gladstone,* 3 volumes (New York, 1969), for an illuminating but too uncritical account of the Grand Old Man and his brand of liberalism. See also the excellent study, *Rosebery* (London, 1963), by Robert Rhodes James; Herman Ausubel, *John Bright: Victorian Reformer* (New York, 1966); Robert Blake, *Disraeli* (New York, 1968); R. S. Churchill, *Winston S. Churchill, The Young Statesman, 1901–1914* (London, 1967); and Herbert Spencer, *An Autobiography,* 2 volumes (London, 1904). *Lloyd George* (London, 1951), by Tom Jones, is probably the best available biography of the last Liberal prime minister. Brief vignettes of "representative" Victorians are attractively presented in Asa Briggs, *Victorian People* (New York, 1965).

No full-scale or definitive history of the Liberal party is in print. Until such a history is written, the reader will find helpful accounts in Hamilton Fyfe, *The British Liberal Party: An Historical Sketch* (London, 1928), Henry Slesser, *A History of the Liberal Party* (London, 1944), and R. B. McCallum, *The Liberal Party from Earl Grey to Asquith* (London, 1963). Valuable readings on specialized topics include two works on the beginnings of the party: Donald Southgate, *The Passing of the Whigs, 1832–1886* (London, 1962), and John Vincent, *The Formation of the Liberal Party 1857–1868* (London, 1966). Other specialized titles are Peter Stansky, *Ambitions and Strategies: The Struggle for Leadership of the Liberal Party in the 1890's* (New York, 1964), Colin Cross, *The Liberals in Power, 1905–1914* (Chester Springs, Pa., 1963), Peter Rowland, *The Last Liberal Governments: The Promised Land, 1905–1910* (New York, 1969) and Paul R. Thompson, *Socialists, Liberals and Labour: The Struggle for London, 1885–1914* (London, 1967). Thompson provides a careful case study of the failure of the Liberals to win the labor vote in the largest city.

For nineteenth-century politics and parties a fine introduction is Eugene Black, *British Politics in the Nineteenth Century* (New York, 1969). Valuable for its treatment of Victorian political organization is volume one of Ivor Bulmer Thomas, *The Growth of the British Party System* (London, 1965). More analytical is volume two of Sir Ivor Jennings' three-volume study, *British Politics* (London, 1961). John F. Harrison edits a well-balanced anthology in *Society and Politics in England, 1780–1960: A Selection of Readings and Comments* (New York, 1965). Norman Gash's *Politics in the Age of Peel* (New York, 1953) is an important study of politicians and the electoral system before mid-century. For the second half of the century, see H. J. Hansham, *Elections and Party Management: Politics in the Time of Disraeli and Gladstone* (London, 1959). For the constitutional dimension, see J. A. Hawgood, "Liberalism and Constitutional Developments," *New Cambridge Modern History* (Cambridge, 1960), Vol. X, and Walter Bagehot's classic, *The English Constitution* (London, 1867).

Simon Maccoby's four volumes (London, 1935–1961) entitled *English Radicalism* offer the most detailed account of radical aspirations in politics. These aspirations are succinctly summarized in his *English Radical Tradition, 1763–1914* (New York, 1957). The changing radicalism of the working class from 1790 to 1832 is treated by E. P. Thompson in *The Making of the English Working Class* (London, 1963). Volume two of Max Beer's *The History of British Socialism* (New York, 1923) discusses the early course of labor politics. See also G. D. H. Cole, *British Working-Class Politics 1832–1914* (New York, 1965), and Henry Pelling, *The Origins of the Labour Party, 1880–1900,* 2nd ed. (New York, 1965). Pelling and W. H. G. Armytage's *A. J. Mundella, 1825–1897: The Liberal Background to the Labour Movement* (London, 1951) are helpful for tracing connections between the Liberal and Labour Parties. For the Fabian Society and its views on liberalism and the state see G. B. Shaw *et al., Fabian Essays in Socialism,* 6th ed., introd. Asa Briggs (New York, 1962), and G. D. H. Cole, *Fabian Socialism* (London, 1943). A. V. Woodworth provides an account of Christian socialism in *Christian Socialism in England* (New York, 1903).

Industrialization and urbanization were twin forces which, along with the democratization of government and society, forced reformulations in liberal attitudes toward the state. Indispensable for the general economic history of the century 1815–1914 is J. H. Clapham's *Economic History of Great Britain,* 3 volumes (Cambridge, 1927–1938). A most satisfactory introduction to economic history, containing the conclusions of more recent research, is W. Ashworth, *Economic History of England, 1870–1939* (New York, 1960). See also W. W. Rostow, *The British Economy of the Nineteenth Century* (New York, 1948), and P. Deane and W. A. Cole, *British Economic Growth* (Cambridge, 1962). Economic and social case studies of London, Leeds, Manchester, and other cities, plus a helpful annotated bibliography, are found in Asa Briggs, *Victorian Cities* (London, 1963). *The History of Birmingham,* 2 volumes (Oxford, 1952), by W. Conrad Gill and Asa Briggs, dissects the political and social structure of the home of municipal socialism. S. G. Checkland writes a carefully documented study in *The Rise of Industrial*

Society in England, 1815–1885 (London, 1964). The most important studies on poverty at the turn of the century are Charles Booth's remarkable seventeen-volume classic, *Life and Labour of the People of London* (London and New York, 1902–1903), and B. Seebohn Rowntree, *Poverty: A Study of Town Life* (London and New York, 1901). *In Darkest England and the Way Out* (London, 1890) is the famous social manifesto of William Booth, founder of the Salvation Army. Equally popular was A. Mearns, *The Bitter Cry of Outcast London,* now in a new edition (Leicester, 1970), by Anthony S. Wohl. Not to be overlooked is W. H. Beveridge, *Unemployment: A Problem of Industry* (New York, 1930).

The pivotal issue of individualism vs. collectivism is treated from the laissez-faire point of view in A. V. Dicey's classic *Lectures on the Relations between Law and Opinion in England* (London, 1914). J. Bartlett Brebner's thesis, in rebuttal, claiming that Bentham was "the archetype of British collectivism," is developed in "Laissez Faire and State Intervention in Nineteenth-Century Britain," *The Journal of Economic History, Supplement VIII* (1948). David Roberts sees Bentham as only of secondary importance in the growth of the state, in "Jeremy Bentham and the Victorian Administrative State," *Victorian Studies,* Vol. II (1959). Bentham is viewed as a believer in the illimitable power of the state, in Gertrude Himmelfarb's assessment, "The Haunted House of Jeremy Bentham," *Ideas in History: Essays Presented to Louis Gottschalk by His Former Students* (Durham, N.C., 1965), edited by Richard Herr and Harold T. Parker. The life of Bentham's most forceful and influential disciple is well recounted in S. E. Finer's biography, *The Life and Times of Sir Edwin Chadwick* (London, 1952). A challenging exposition of the counterbalance of individualism and communal institutions in mid-Victorian England is *The Age of Equapoise* (New York, 1964), by W. L. Burn. A case for the origins of the administrative revolution in the administrative process is offered by Oliver MacDonagh in *A Pattern of Government Growth, 1800–1860: The Passenger Acts and their Enforcement* (London, 1961). Roger Prouty examines the administration of a department in *The Transformation of the Board of Trade, 1830–1855* (London, 1957). See also David Roberts, *Victorian Origins of the Welfare State* (Oxford, 1960) for his contribution to the historical debate over the Victorian revolution in government and the influence of utilitarianism on English life and political thought.